MEDIA vs TRUMP
JIHAD

THE CORRUPT ELECTION

LOU LAWRENCE

TRUMP'S VICTORY

THE BOLT FROM THE BLUE

DONALD TRUMP'S VICTORY WAS A SHOCK FOR HILLARY AND DEMOCRATS, BUT IT WAS NOT AN UPSET. THE AMERICAN PUBLIC DEMANDED A CHANGE IN WASHINGTON, AND TRUMP WAS THAT CHANGE.

DESPITE THE ILLEGAL ACTIONS BY THE OBAMA ADMINISTRATION, DONALD TRUMP WAS ELECTED THE 45TH PRESIDENT OF THE UNITED STATES.

CONTENTS

BOOKS BY LOU LAWRENCE

AVAILABLE ON AMAZON BOOKS

BAILOUT? BALONEY!
BANKRUPTCIES OF CHRYSLER AND GM

TOO BIG TO FAIL SNAFU
WALL STREET BAILOUTS

RANSOM OLDS
THE FORGOTTEN AUTO TITAN

ART HISTORY
YESTERDAY-TODAY

ART FOR KIDS
FAMOUS ART & ARTISTS

DIABETES HANDBOOK
TEN COMMANDMENTS FOR DIABETICS

MEDIA vs TRUMP JIHAD
THE CORRUPT ELECTION

PREFACE

The Obama administration attempted to fix the 2016 presidential election; the first time in history the government interfered in an election. Donald Trump claimed the election was *rigged,* and he was right on. The FBI and CIA were involved, and the DOJ directed the illegal activities.

The media and Democrats continue to claim a Trump connection with Russia, despite the fact that the Russia-Trump dossier was proven false. Two years of FBI investigations have found no evidence that Donald Trump was involved with Russia, and a yearlong House Intel Committee investigation found no Trump connection.

Hillary Clinton paid $12.4 million to an unsavory political research firm Fusion GPS to obtain dirt on Donald Trump. Fusion produced 17 memos called the *dossier* claiming that Trump colluded with Russia to damage Hillary's candidacy. The dossier was analyzed and immediately proven a fabrication. However, Democrats and the media jihad used the dossier to attack Donald Trump. The supposed Russia-Trump issue became the prime tool for the anti-Trump crowd. The dubious dossier became the primary instrument for attacking Trump, despite the document being untrue, and paid for by his political opponent.

The possibility of rigging a presidential election is slight because the voting is decentralized, and the votes are not part of the internet. There is no evidence that any foreign country has ever fixed a presidential election.

The possibility of Russia interfering in the 2016 election became the main talking point in the election. However, the media ignored that President Obama used taxpayer money attempting to oust Prime Minister Netanyahu in 2015. The U.S. is also guilty of fixing elections in South America, and attempted to overthrow Castro in Cuba. The CIA also started a coup in South Korea during the Vietnam War. Evidently, interfering in elections is common.

The media failed to make an issue of Obama's illegal actions in 2015, and the covert operations in foreign elections were ignored, but the false claim that Trump hurt Hillary's chances in 2016 became top news.

The media picked Hillary as their candidate for president when she left the secretary of state position in January 2013. The election of a female president was the main objective. The press was so enamored of Hillary they failed to recognize her weaknesses. She had 40 years of baggage that would not go away, and her accomplishments were almost nonexistent.

When Donald Trump announced he was running for president on June 15, 2015, the media immediately attacked him – he was a threat to their favorite candidate. The assaults against Trump became so vicious the media appeared to be in a religion crusade or jihad against Trump.

The media pulled out all stops in an attempt to kill Trump's chances, including false reports on almost everything he had ever done or accomplished in business. His family was attacked with savage comments, and TV comedians made fun of everything he did. The jihad was getting out of hand.

The media has a reputation of winning every personal attack battle, but they underestimated Donald Trump. Trump began using the term *fake news* to describe the press releases, and the name stuck.

The meaning of the expression is *reporting bogus or counterfeit information.* Fake news is not journalism; it consists of data presented as accurate, but has no basis for accuracy– it is precisely wrong. The media fake news reports are now the norm, rather than the exception; many fake news reports are actually delusional.

The average news watcher recognizes the news bias, and takes the fake news with a grain of salt. Trump immediately recognized the media jihad, and began tweeting items for the media to chase; he baited reporters with his tweets, and the jihad took the bait. Trump began winning the media battle.

The media assault on Republican candidates was limited to Trump; the early favorites, Jeb Bush and Scott Walker, were left alone. There were 17 Republican candidates for president, and all were capable individuals, but for some unknown reason, Donald Trump received the media attention.

Not only was the media against Trump, the FBI was doing everything possible to sabotage his candidacy. For the first time in history, a Federal Government agency attempted to fix a presidential election. FBI Director Comey was

determined to help Hillary get elected, and the *help* involved illegal spying on Trump's campaign office. Comey was fired in 2017 for his actions.

Despite the dossier being a fairy tale, the Democrats and media continued with their attacks on Trump for supposed Russia collusion. There was no evidence of any Trump connection with Russia, and the entire Russia claim was hogwash. The FBI investigated the Trump- Russia issue for two years and found no connection with Russia. The Mueller Special Counsel also failed to find evidence of any Trump collusion.

There were questionable elections in the 1800s, but the 2016 presidential election was the most corrupt in history. A former FBI agent exposed the illegal FBI Spygate, and Congress began an investigation of the FBI.

The media jihad was determined to damage Trump, and used no holds barred tactics throughout the primaries, the election, and the post-election periods. Trump used the term *fake news* as his way of fighting back, and it was successful. The fake news reports were so bizarre that voters sided with Donald Trump. The public could read between the lines, and recognized the media bias.

The media have attacked presidents since the days of George Washington, but Trump is the only president to win the media battle. He baited the press, and they chased his tweets with a passion and appeared foolish.

The silent majority movement was tired of the Washington do-nothing politicians, and wanted to take their country back. The mid-term elections had kicked many incumbents out of office, and the voters demanded change. Evidently, Hillary failed to read the tealeaves, and her campaign platform was to continue with Obama policies.

The country was still in the 2008 housing recession in 2016. There were nine million out of work, homeowners were under water on their mortgages, and there were forty-eight million on food stamps. The GDP growth rate was less than two percent – a recession-era growth.

Voters certainly recognized the economy was a disaster, but Hillary and the DNC continued with the Obama failed economy policies. Hillary must have been drinking the Obama Kool-Aid, because the eight years of the Obama economy were the worst since the Great Depression of the 1930s.

CHAPTER ONE
POLITICAL ENVIRONMENT

The political environment in Washington in 2016 was like two Americas with Democrats and Republicans at war. The non-stop media attacks on Donald Trump became the prime element of the political scene.

The media did not attack the other sixteen Republican candidates. Donald Trump was the only target of the media jihad, and this has never been explained. The media fake news jihad against Trump was so crazy that most voters simply tuned them out.

Watergate

The 1972 Watergate spying scandal was a disaster, but the FBI spying on Trump's campaign office 44 years later was worse. The FBI Spygate was illegal because a government agency attempted to fix an election. Watergate involved Nixon followers going out of their way to sort through Democrat papers, but government agencies were not directly involved in 1972.

The political environment included Democrats accusing Republicans of racism whenever they disagreed with their programs. During President Obama's eight years, he continually attacked the Republican Party as being racist. Obama failed to check history with his racism claims.

In 1854, the Republican Party promoted anti-slavery, and picked Abraham Lincoln as the Republican nominee for president in 1860. Democrats remained pro-slavery, and even supported the Ku Klux Klan. The Democrats have changed history with the racism claim.

President Obama claimed he had fixed the recession, but the economy was still a disaster. Unemployment of nine million, 48 million on food stamps, and a 1.7% GDP certainly proved the recession was continuing. Voters knew the economy was in the tank, but Democrats ignored the issue. The 2008 housing recession was the worst financial crisis since the Great Depression. Ben Bernanke said the fall of 2008 was the worst financial period in the nation's history, including the Great Depression.

President Obama made *jobs* his priority in his first State of the Union address; he talked a good game, but he failed - unemployment increased. During his eight years, the number of people working *decreased by 5%.*

The GDP growth rate never reached 3% during his reign – the first time this ever happened to a president. The GDP had *averaged* 5% in prior post-recession periods.

Congress caused the 2008 housing recession with legislation (that failed) to increase home ownership for minorities. Home mortgages no longer required a down payment, and credit ratings were ignored; only a signature was required to obtain a mortgage.

When the new homeowners could not make their monthly payments, fifteen million foreclosures resulted. The number of minorities owning homes actually declined when Congress interfered in the housing market.

President Obama continually reported that he inherited the financial crisis, but he was in the Senate when the legislation was passed. The main issue was that he failed to fix the problem. Homeowners lost 50% of their home equity in the recession, and they were still under water on their home mortgages when Obama left office.

President Obama attempted to *pump up* the economy, but the recession continued until Trump was elected. The eight-year housing recession was nearly as long as the thirteen-year Great Depression.

GDP is the most accurate measurement of the economy, and while Obama touted his supposed economic improvements, GDP growth of 1.7% was the worst in history. The President also made jobs his top priority, but job growth was non-existent during his eight years.

Hillary's plan to continue the Obama policies was a serious error. She failed to recognize that voters had tired of the weak economy and job losses. Evidently, Hillary forgot the James Carville warning *it's the economy, stupid.*

The economy was a problem and the silent majority was angry with Washington for doing nothing about unemployment. Donald Trump knew that the economy was a disaster, and developed a plan that included tax cuts, trade changes, eliminating Obama regulations, and job creation. Hillary' platform was to leave everything alone.

It was amazing that Hillary, the DNC, and the mainstream media failed to pay attention to the mid-term elections. Voters wanted a change, but Democrats ignored it. The unemployed and underemployed surely knew the economy was a major problem, but Hillary failed to listen to voters.

The media dislike of Trump was so intense that an anti-Trump jihad started. With the polls reporting a huge Hillary lead, the media used the poll data as gospel to attack Trump, and beat the drums for Hillary's nomination and election. The drive-by media was obviously biased, and their prejudice led to a *jihad* to destroy Donald Trump.

Donald Trump did not trust the poll data; his comment was *I don't need a poll to make a decision.* Quite different from President Obama who had never made a decision in his two years as a senator; he voted *present* on legislation; *never* a yes or no vote.

Trump recognized that voters were hurting with high unemployment, and criticized the reported 5% unemployment rate promoted by the government. His estimate of unemployment was 20%. The government unemployment rate was obviously wrong; the people laid off, but working part time, were counted as employed.

Donald Trump was the only presidential candidate to make jobs and the economy key campaign issues. Voters considered job losses the main issue, and Trump's business experience allowed him to see the problem. His plans to reduce Obama business regulations, approve the Keystone Pipeline, fix trade, and reduce taxes, would create jobs. Hillary was asleep at the wheel; she had no plan to increase jobs.

Obamacare cost had doubled, and Trump demanded a new health plan; Hillary disagreed. Not a single Republican voted for Obamacare, when the legislation was passed in 2010. The Democrats pushed the *affordable health-care* legislation through Congress without reading the 20,000-page charter. By 2015, the cost of Obamacare had doubled in many states, and the infamous commitment by President Obama that *you can keep your doctor* was a *whopper.*

Republicans introduced a bill to repeal the costly health-care legislation in 2015, but Democrats stood fast and rejected the act. The excessive cost was not a priority for Democrats, and they continued to claim the *affordable health care* legislation was working, and was Obama's greatest accomplishment.

John McCain was one of the few Republicans who voted *against* the repeal of Obamacare. The repeal was one of Donald Trump's key campaign promises, and health care cost in Arizona was the highest in the nation. McCain was an enemy of Donald Trump, and he voted to hurt Trump rather than help his state.

Trade imbalance had been a serious problem decades, but Washington politicians had ignored the trillion dollar trade problem. Attorneys, as politicians, simply did not know how to fix trade imbalance, and U.S. companies suffered with a loss of business, plant closures, and job losses.

The movement of U.S. plants and jobs out of the country had continued for nearly seventy years. Foreign countries manipulated currency exchange rates to make their products cheaper in the U.S. and American firms moved plants to other countries to stay in business.

Politicians evidently did not know what to do, and failed to correct the trade problem even though their states lost jobs when the plants moved out. The lack of business experience is common in Washington; most politicians are attorneys, and *Business 101* is not included in the law school curriculum.

Japan began using exchange rates as a tool for trade in the 1950s. A Toyota cost less in the U.S. than it did in Japan – an impossibility when freight and duty are considered. During that time, the Japanese yen was 300-1 for the U.S. dollar; a Big Mac would cost fifteen cents at that rate. Evidently, the effect of currency exchange rates is beyond the IQ of Washington politicians.

In addition to quality issues, the exchange rate disparity cost millions of automotive jobs. The exchange rate issue was proven to be the causal factor when many other U.S. firms were attacked by the Japanese where quality was not such an issue. Heavy equipment companies like Caterpillar, camera makers like Kodak, and electronics firms, lost a large share of their markets, and most closed their U.S. plants.

US-China trade deficit

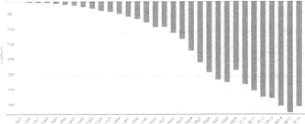
In 20 years, the trade deficit between the United States in China went from near zero to $347 billion in 2016.

The trade deficit with China has increased dramatically over the past fifteen years and reached $375 billion in 2017. The overall U.S. trade deficit increased 12% to nearly $600 billion.

Past presidents and Congress had completely ignored the trade imbalance problem for decades. President Obama also failed to do anything about the issue during his eight years.

Donald Trump was an executive and knew that trade imbalance was a serious job issue. The main difference between Trump and politicians is he knows how to run a business, and unbelievably, the government is a business. Donald Trump was the only one of 22 candidates who made *trade* one of his campaign promises.

The Japanese government supported their carmakers, while the U.S. legislators provided no help for the Big Three. Ford CEO Alan Mulally said, *Washington treats U.S. automakers like drug runners.* For some reason, politicians are hostile toward the U.S. carmakers, and spent three months criticizing the industry. Their animosity toward the automotive business in the 2008 hearings resulted in a vote against an auto bailout. GM and Chrysler were driven into bankruptcy – the opposite of a bailout.

Donald Trump was the only presidential candidate who understood the trade imbalance impact on business, the economy, and jobs. Trump criticized current trade agreements, and called the trade negotiators *idiots*. Trump's *Made in America* theme hit home with voters.

Trump's business expertise was the main difference between the presidential candidates. Hillary had no business experience, and out of the 16 other Republican candidates, only Carley Fiorina had been in the business environment.

The other candidates were politicians. Politicians make speeches; business executives make problems go away.

Trump's positive attitude, and ability to take *center stage* in all situations, made him the leading Republican candidate. This was truly amazing – Trump overshadowed Jeb Bush, Scott Walker, and Ted Cruz – the early favorites for the Republican nomination.

Bernie Sanders and Donald Trump were threats to Hillary; Bernie was defeating Hillary in 40% of their contests, and Donald Trump was winning the Republican primaries. The Clinton machine had taken care of threats in the past, and a plan for Bernie and Trump was developing.

Bernie Sanders is a Socialist with plans to give away the store to everybody without talking about budget deficits or the national debt. Hillary attempted to match Bernie's giveaway programs in their meetings, but could never match his giveaways. Bernie Sanders, the *unknown candidate,* became a threat to Hillary.

While Donald Trump was called *non-presidential* by the media, he was cleaning house in the primaries, and was likely the Republican nominee; he was another threat for Hillary.

Hillary may not be too smart, but she is a dangerous politician. Bill Clinton is smarter, and is a cutthroat politician. With this team working against them, Bernie and Trump needed steel protection to survive the Clinton machine.

Immigration had been a political problem for years, and the reason it continued without any resolution was that Democrats were demanding amnesty for illegals. The root cause of the demand was that the Democratic Party wanted to increase their voting base with illegal immigrants. Voting by illegals is against the law, but Democrat politicians conveniently ignore the law. The media supports illegals voting, but never mentions that it is against the law.

The Hillary Immigration Plan

When the media cover the Republican immigration position, the party is always reported to be *un-American.* The fact is that Republicans simply want the immigration laws enforced. Democrats, the media, and even the courts, ignore the immigration laws.

President Trump has the authority to protect the country from criminals and drug cartels, but the courts prevented his executive order from going into effect.

Obama issued executive orders in 2012 to prevent deportation of illegal immigrants. The DACA Policy (Deferred Action for Childhood Arrivals) was illegal, but Obama believed that future presidents would not object because of the political fallout. President Obama underestimated Donald Trump; he was not interested in political correctness.

President Obama's *Dreamers* program demanded illegals awaiting citizenship be granted amnesty, and be allowed to vote. Obama created serious immigration problems during his eight years, and his belief was that Republicans would refuse to overturn DACA and Dreamers because of the politics involved.

The DACA and Dreamers legislation has not been approved, and there is no chance that the political parties can agree on immigration; their basic issues are too far apart. Democrats do not think as Americans, only as partisan politicians. Democrats even shut the government down in 2018 over DACA; they put illegal immigrants ahead of American citizens – unbelievable.

While the political parties always have different opinions, the number of major disagreements was higher than normal in the 2016 election. President Obama's policies had created a wide division between Democrats and Republicans, and this division was evident in the campaign platforms of Hillary and Trump. Hillary campaigned for illegal immigration, while Trump demanded that immigration laws be enforced. The primaries and election would highlight these differences.

The media crusade against Donald Trump was vicious, and they ignored the other Republican candidates; Trump was their only target. The early Republican favorites Jeb Bush and Scott Walker did not receive the ferocious attacks, and the other Republican candidates went scot-free.

The vicious media attacks included personal assassination attempts, and attacks on his family, including his twelve-year old son. The media jihad against Trump has never been explained, but the crusade continued throughout the primaries, the election, and after the election. The media versus Trump movement is similar to the Islamic jihad against non-believers in that it is an organized *fight to the death* effort.

After Trump was elected President, Democrats and the media jihad were determined to damage the President. The Russia-Trump claim was the main topic.

The Washington scene was complex in the election period. The nation was deeply divided on most issues, and the negative economic condition made the situation even worse. The silent majority had expressed their anger with Washington politicians in the 2010 and 2014 mid-term elections by voting many out of office.

However, Hillary and the DNC failed to recognize the significance of the mid-term elections. They ignored the silent majority voters. Donald Trump paid no attention to the media or the crazy polls, but did pay attention to the voters at his rallies. He soon determined that voters were unhappy with Washington and wanted a change. He was to be that change.

The media jihad against Donald Trump is the worst in history; never before has the media taken such a strong position against a candidate for president. The continuous personal assassinations were bad enough, but the attacks on his wife and children were deplorable.

Democrat politicians jumped on the media anti-Trump bandwagon; the tag team Schumer and Pelosi went out of their way to criticize Donald Trump. However, most of their claims were questionable, and many were even ridiculous.

Newspapers in the 1790s criticized George Washington unmercifully, even condemning his military ability. This was a laughable attack since Washington was the hero of the Revolutionary War, but journalists often have trouble with the truth – even 230 years ago.

Washington was elected unanimously to two terms as President, but refused a third term as he was *disinclined to be buffeted in public print by infamous scribblers.* Washington's criticism of the media was mild compared to later presidents.

Thomas Jefferson, our third president, was also attacked by the media and said: *Nothing can be believed which is written in a newspaper.* Jefferson also used words similar to Trump's fake news by saying: *Newspapers are polluted vehicles of falsehood and error.* The media continued to criticize presidents through the years; Richard Nixon considered the media his mortal enemy. Bill Clinton often criticized the press, and George W. Bush used profanity when discussing the media.

The truth is often missing in the media attacks on Trump; as Will Rogers said *If truth were injected into politics, there would be no politics.* The media jihad is so obviously false that the public ignores it. The FBI, the Clinton machine, the polls, and the media, all went as far as they could to destroy Donald Trump, but he survived. It takes a tough person to survive that onslaught, and Trump was up to the battle.

Donald Trump's experience dealing with the tough New York construction unions prepared him for the unsavory political attacks during the election. Politics is also a tough business because of the two-faced politicians. The Will Rogers' comment on politicians: *A fool and his money will soon be elected.*

The weak economy hurt Hillary in the election; the anemic GDP growth rate of 1.7 % was a disaster. President Obama attempted to give excuses for the poor economy, but voters ignored his rhetoric. He always began by claiming the economy was not his fault since the 2008 recession started before he was elected.

The recession did begin before his election, but his excuse was splitting hairs. He was a senator when Congress passed legislation that caused the recession, so he certainly helped create the worst economic period in the nation's history. The 2008 recession was worse than the Great Depression according to Ben Bernanke.

The government claimed the recession ended in June 2009, but the American public disagreed. Homeowners lost 50% of their home equity during the 2008 housing recession, and most were still under water on their home loans.

Despite President Obama's jobs program introduced in his first State of the Union address, the number working declined 5% during his presidency. There were nine million standing in unemployment lines in 2016, very similar to the Great Depression in the 1930s. The only difference was that the unemployed were not standing on corners selling apples. However, there were forty-eight million on food stamps.

The Obama economy was simply *bad,* and the government was not doing anything to make it better. The media ignored the economy issue by continuing their support for Hillary; evidently, they believed she would be the savior for the financial disaster. This idea had little credibility since Hillary's campaign platform was to continue with the Obama economic policies.

Even though the 2008-2009 recession was ancient history in 2016, workers remembered the plant closures and layoffs; *the scare of a layoff never goes away.* The government claim that the recession ended after 18 months was a dream and an attempt to prove that President Obama's polices had ended the crises. This was a fairy tale that only the Democrats and the media believed.

Also forgotten was that the 2008 housing recession was caused by congressional politicians voting for affordable housing for minorities. The *politically correct* legislators caused 200,000 small businesses and the auto industry to go into bankruptcy with their legislation.

The deep recession caused bank failures, and small companies were unable to borrow funds to stay in business. Vehicle sales fell 40%, and the Big Three ran out of working capital to pay their workers and suppliers. The automobile industry, with three million workers went bankrupt.

Chrysler and General Motors were forced into bankruptcy in April and June of 2009. The Treasury had bailed out Wall Street and the banks with $14 *trillion* two weeks after the Lehman bankruptcy on September 15, 2008, but rejected the auto request for a $35 *billion* loan. There was something wrong with that picture.

Congress voted *against* an auto bailout after three months of *studies.* The negative vote received little media attention, because the politicians were claiming they bailed out the automobile industry. How Congress could take credit for saving the carmakers when Chrysler and GM were driven into bankruptcy is anybody's guess. Evidently, attorneys don't understand the difference between bankruptcy and a bailout. The media also touted the *bailout* of the automobile industry, but fake news had proven those characters to be less than bright.

The government propaganda worked because most Americans believe that there was a bailout of the auto industry, despite the Senate voting 52-35 *against* a bailout. President Obama also claimed credit for bailing out the auto industry, despite voting against an auto bailout when he took office in January 2009.

Obama's actions on the auto industry were even worse than Congress. His plan after the election of 2008 was to cover up the $14 trillion fraudulent gift to Wall Street and 800 banks, by studying the auto business until the public anger with the Wall Street fiasco died down.

After three months of Congressional Hearings on the auto industry, Obama began the five-month Rattner *study* as soon as he took office in January 2009. Steven Rattner, a Wall Street type, had never been in an auto plant, and his team of Wall Street *auto experts* knew nothing about the automobile industry; some didn't even own a car.

Rattner fired the CEO of General Motors, the first time the government had ever fired the CEO of a business. He also literally *gave* Chrysler to a foreign company, Fiat. This gift of the third largest U.S. auto manufacturer to Fiat, a company that had dropped out of the American market because of poor quality, was never explained. Auto industry pundits called Fiat *Fix It Again Tony* because of their quality problems.

Rattner was a political appointee who was forced to end his job as the *car czar* when he was indicted by the State of New York for fraud. Rattner paid a $10 million fine to avoid jail.

Congress blamed the 2008-2009 housing recession on business greed, but the recession was caused by legislation to increase minority home ownership. The legislation created a housing boom that burst in 2007 with fifteen million foreclosures.

The government minority-housing program failed when the homeowners could not make their mortgage payments, but legislators still took credit for the *affordable housing* fiasco. The housing legislation failed; the result was less minority home ownership.

Congress refused to accept responsibility for the housing debacle; Senate Majority Leader Mitch McConnell stated *We had nothing to do with the mortgage disaster.* The lack of accountability in Washington is amazing.

Most recognize that the government is slow in making decisions, but taking eight months to *study* the auto industry was ridiculous. A first year accounting student could have found that working capital was the problem. The recession caused vehicle sales to drop 40%, and the carmakers ran out of working capital; the firms did not have the cash to pay their workers and suppliers. No company can survive a 40% drop in revenue in one year whether they make cars or computers.

The Big Three were bankrupt by November 2008 and the government was required to loan working capital to the automakers to keep their doors open during the eight months of studies.

The total working capital required during the three months of Congressional Hearings, and the five months of the Obama-Rattner *study* was $60 billion. The $79 billion loaned to Chrysler and General Motors received extensive news coverage, but the media failed to report that 75%

of the loan was necessary for working capital to keep the two automakers open during the eight months of government *studies.* The politicians did not *study* Wall Street before giving $14 trillion to the financial community. The entire automotive study process was a sham.

The government-caused recession had killed vehicle sales and the automakers needed working capital to survive. Evidently, Congress failed to understand the need for working capital, and held Congressional Hearings for three months criticizing the auto executives for their inability to overcome the housing recession. Congress even refused to accept that the 2008 recession had caused the drop in auto sales.

The so-called *bailout* of Wall Street cost $14 trillion of taxpayer money, and Treasury Secretary, Henry Paulson created the disaster. He panicked when Lehman Brothers filed for bankruptcy on September 15, 2008. Paulson gave trillions to Wall Street, over 800 banks, and hundreds of mortgage companies. Sadly, he ignored *Main Street.*

An example of the Wall Street greed was Goldman Sachs. Goldman never lost money during the recession, yet received $30 billion in bailout money. The firm used it for bonuses; even secretaries received $500,000 in bonuses. Main Street and Detroit got zip.

The public is unaware that 75% of the $79 billion loaned to automotive was necessary to keep the carmakers' doors open during the eight month-government studies. The balance was the cost of the two bankruptcies.

After Congress voted against an auto bailout, President Bush approved a $17.4 billion loan for Chrysler and GM on December 19, 2008 to keep their doors open until President Obama took office. The loan was only a Band Aid because of the five-month Rattner study fiasco.

The Wall Street bailout was hidden by the government, and received little media attention, but the supposed *auto bailout* was front-page news for months. The amazing thing was that the government propaganda worked. The public forgot the $14 *trillion* gift to Wall Street, but remembered the government loan of $79 *billion* to the automakers. The media fed the public the fake news continuously for two years.

President Obama was touting saving the U.S. auto industry, despite driving Chrysler and General Motors into bankruptcy. Obama also used the auto bailout theme to win the 2012 election; evidently, voters did not realize that bankruptcy was the *opposite* of a bailout.

The media reported the $79 *billion* auto loan, but ignored the $14 *trillion* government gift to Wall Street and the banks. Politicians also refused to accept that legislation caused the housing recession that drove vehicle sales to the lowest level in thirty years.

The auto loan request for a $35 billion loan was peanuts compared to the $14 trillion *bailout* of Wall Street and banks.

The tragedy would have been avoided if the legislators had done their job. The responsibility was to protect one of the largest industries in the country, not to drive two of the Big Three into bankruptcy. If the government actions during the recession were made into a Broadway comedy, nobody would believe it.

The 2008 recession set the stage for the eight years of the dismal Obama economy. Obama had no fixes for the recession, and the hard times continued during his presidency. Proof that the economy was still in the recession during the Obama reign was the *$40 payday in 2011 and 2012.* President Obama approved cancelling the FICA withholding tax to pay workers forty dollars for three months – what a joke.

Obama's big payday was a ridiculous effort to show the nation that his administration was helping during the hard times of the recession. Trump's tax cuts in 2017 paid thousands in bonuses to families – quite a difference.

The 2008 recession continued until Donald Trump was elected in November 2016; once Trump was elected, the stock market boomed, and the economy finally improved. The media jihad actually refused to report the dramatic improvement in the economy.

The drive-by media were in Obama's corner and refused to report the disastrous economic crisis during his eight years. Workers were suffering but the media ignored the situation. The economy was a major factor with voters in the 2016 election, and the idiom *it's the economy, stupid* was still the message. The media was focused on the women issue, and completely missed the silent majority anger about jobs and the anemic economy.

The fact that the 2008 housing recession was caused by government legislation to increase minority home ownership was ignored. Political correctness did not allow politicians to criticize the actions that caused the worst economic period in the nation's history.

The tragedy was that the *affordable housing* legislation not only failed to *increase* minority home ownership, but the fifteen million foreclosures actually *decreased* home ownership. Fifteen million of the new homeowners went into foreclosure when they were unable to make their mortgage payments. Congress refused to accept any responsibility for the debacle and blamed the housing recession on speculators.

Congress caused the recession, immediately bailed out friends on Wall Street with $14 trillion of taxpayer money, but refused to bailout Main Street. The public is unaware of the trickery because the Treasury hid the Wall Street bailout. There is no accountability for politicians, and they always deny responsibility.

President Obama made jobs his first priority in his State of the Union speeches, but he ignored the fact that his oratory failed to create any jobs. The number of people in the workforce declined by five percent during the Obama eight years.

The jobs program was a total failure. During his presidency, Obama continually claimed he had improved the economy, and saved the nation from the disastrous housing recession. The nine million unemployed had trouble with the claim.

Despite all economic indicators showing the economy to be in a tailspin, Hillary and the DNC were continuing with the Obama policies in the Democrat campaign platform. The millions whose mortgages were still under water, and the huge number of unemployed certainly understood the economy was still in the recession.

The government was reporting a five percent unemployment rate, but the real number was much higher. Donald Trump discounted the government rate, and he was right. The millions of *underemployed* were counted as employed, and the resulting government unemployment rate was lower than actual.

Voters were becoming believers in Trump's campaign promises; they had enough of political double-talk. The general feeling of the working class was that politicians considered them permanent Democrats and would not change, but voters wanted to take their country back. The economy was a key factor in the 2016 election, but Hillary and the DNC failed to recognize the problem. Hillary had no plan to fix the economy, or reduce the trade imbalance.

Trump received 15% more working class votes than Mitt Romney in 2012; even union members were for Trump. At the Detroit Trump rallies, UAW members sat next to auto executives. UAW management failed to attend the rallies, but UAW workers were there. Trump's theme of *Make America Great Again* was popular with the working class.

Donald Trump used his *draining the swamp* idea during his campaign to rid Washington of bureaucrats. The concept is popular with voters, but politicians are against draining the swamp; attacking their job security does not fit with their career plan. Most will stay in Washington as long as they can be reelected, and feel that Trump should not be upsetting the apple cart.

The average voter does not realize that there are 487 members of Congress, and many stay on the government payroll as long as they can. The legislative section is the largest branch of the government, and the most inefficient. The 487 politicians make speeches, but rarely get anything done. Congress *investigated* the Benghazi tragedy for four years without any action; but there were tons of TV speeches.

Congress has two chambers – the Senate with 50 members, and the House of Representatives with 437 members. There are currently 51 Republican senators, and 49 Democrats; the House consists of 240 Republicans and 197 Democrats. A few members of Congress claim to be for term limits when asked, but in reality none of the group desire any limit on their time in office. The Founding Fathers did not specify term limits in the Constitution, but over time, the three branches of the government have arrived at three different term limits.

The Supreme Court judges have lifetime tenure, although Article Three of the Constitution only states that judges can remain in office *during good behavior.* Of course, the court has ruled that this means lifetime jobs.

Roosevelt was elected president four times, and Congress quickly passed an Amendment to the Constitution limiting presidents to two four-year terms. However, the Amendment did not include Congress, so legislators can stay in office as long as they can be reelected.

Congress should be limited to two terms to break up the bureaucracy in Washington, but politicians will never vote for term limits. The Constitution does allow the states to make a change if 75% of the states agree, so there is an alternative to Congress refusing term limits. One can only hope.

A revolution has started. Twelve states have approved an amendment to limit congressional terms, and thirty-four states have the change under study in their legislature. If thirty-eight states agree on term limits, many politicians will be looking for a job.

The political world could finally change in Washington. The term limit revolution has received little media attention, but there is definitely a movement in progress. Politicians will never agree with Trump's *drain the swamp* plan; but if the 75% of the states vote for term limits, the problem would be solved. Legislators would no longer be *permanent politicians;* possibly the budget could be balanced, and the national debt reduced for our grandchildren.

The government needs changing, and the voting public recognized the need to change Washington. Trump's plan was just the ticket. Politicians ignored that Americans were fed up with Washington politicians.

The Democrats and media jihad complained that Donald Trump was not a politician, but that is precisely what the nation needs. Will Rogers said *who started the idea that a president must be a politician instead of a businessman.*

The public opinion polls had shown politicians were ranked below used car salesmen, but they ignored the issue. Evidently, they believed they were immune to public opinion. Washington politicians certainly were not supporting the drain the swamp proposal.

The Washington climate is one of bureaucratic apathy and negligence. The poor economy and job losses were major voter issues in 2016, but the politicians in Washington were doing nothing about it. Congress is continually deadlocked, and never gets anything done; legislation is kicked back and forth between the House and the Senate.

The annual budget is another problem; the budget has been balanced only five times in the past 60 years. Congressional spending is a huge problem; legislators continue to spend more than tax revenues take in. Politicians spend $500 *billion* more than the budget *every year.*

The financial performance of Congress is atrocious; the legislators do nothing about reducing spending and lowering the national debt.

Lobbyists demand repayment for their campaign contributions, and congressional spending satisfies the demand. Congress revised the nation's budget system in 1974, and since then budget deficits and the national debt have increased dramatically because a *baseline budget* is used to establish the base for annual budgets. The entire government budget system is broken.

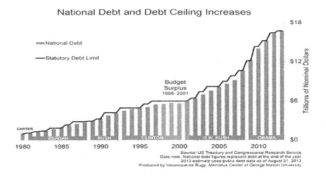

National Debt and Debt Ceiling Increases

During World War II, the debt increased to $250 billion, but excessive spending caused the debt to increase to $10 *trillion* by 2008. The national debt doubled to $20 trillion during the Obama reign; an unbelievable lack of fiscal responsibility.

A big part of the budget problem is the budget process itself. The 1974 legislation that allowed Congress to use a baseline budget process created a big problem. Most industrial firms use a zero-base budget method in which all expenses must be justified every year. The baseline budget system keeps all prior-year expenses in the following year budget. Nothing is questioned, so all *pork is included* in the next year's budget. This ridiculous budget system has been used for the past 44 years, and the national debt has grown to $20 trillion.

Congress allows the prior year budget to increase every year for inflation and population growth, and the increases amounts to 10%. Private firms do not allow budget increases for inflation; management is expected to increase efficiency. If companies increased the budget 10% every year, they would go into bankruptcy. The government sails along with the 10% annual increases every year, and never demands more efficiency or spending reductions.

Congress obviously has no interest in a balanced budget because spending continues to increase. Congress spent *$666 billion more* than the budget in 2017, despite the 10% increase in the budget – unbelievable.

In addition to the weak economy, the public was angry with Congress doing nothing to reduce spending. The budget deficits continued, and the national debt doubled during Obama's eight years.

In addition to the bleak economy, foreign policy was the worst in history. The Obama Iran program raised concern throughout the world. Israel's Benjamin Netanyahu was so concerned that he made speeches against the Iran *deal* to Congress and the United Nations.

President Obama sent $1.7 billion to Iran in an *unmarked plane* as a payoff for releasing three American captives. This was against the nation's policy of not negotiating with terrorists, and was an indication that he would do anything to save his *legacy.* While Hillary reported the Obama-Iran, *deal* was the best thing since *sliced-bread;* Trump continued to criticize the agreement.

The Iran nuclear threat was a critical foreign policy issue since Iran had stockpiles of nuclear material, and President Obama was under pressure to eliminate the nuclear threat. Obama touted the *Iran deal* as a major accomplishment even though it did nothing to control Iran's development of nuclear weapons.

The Iran and North Korean nuclear threats continued without significant U.S. sanctions, and the Middle East was in turmoil. The nation had spent over seven *trillion* in the Middle East with no improvement. American allies had written off the nation in managing the world's disputes.

Hillary Clinton was the secretary of state during Obama's first term, but did nothing about the Iran and North Korea nuclear threats. Many reported that she was responsible for the worst foreign policy mistakes in fifty years.

Even though Hillary touted her experience at State during the campaign, she only increased the travel budget; her mistakes were catching up with her.

Donald Trump was critical of the Obama foreign policies, particularly the failed Obama *line in the sand* with Syria. After Trump was elected he sent missiles via express mail to Syria twice in his first 16 months over the use of chemical weapons against women and children.

President Trump also changed the world by negotiating a stop to North Korea's missile program. Obama sent Dennis Rodman, the *old* Detroit Piston basketball star to North Korea, but his trips to North Korea were a joke, and nothing was accomplished.

North Korea was sending missiles over Japan to prove nuclear power, and the entire world, including the U.S., was concerned. President Trump began tightening controls on shipments to North Korea that damaged their economy. North Korea's leader Kim Jong Un bragged in a televised speech that *The U.S. should know that the button for nuclear weapons is on my table.* President Trump immediately replied *I too have a nuclear button, and mine is much bigger and*

more powerful than his, and my button works.
President Trump forced China and other nations
to stop shipping material to North Korea, and the
U.S. did the same. North Korea was indeed
hurting. By mid-April, President Trump won the
battle with Kim Jong Un; Kim stopped firing
missiles and stopped nuclear development.

This was an amazing accomplishment, similar
to the fall of the Berlin Wall. News watchers did
not get the stunning news because the
mainstream media refused to cover it. Fake
news took priority.

Obama and Hillary's *do nothing* foreign policy
was a disaster. Donald Trump's negotiating skills
are unmatched, and he uses this skill to succeed
in foreign policy, trade, and the economy. His
strong tactics with North Korea, the increase in
the economy and his trade policies have finally
tipped the scale in the favor of the U.S.

The Clintons, the DNC, and the FBI would
make the 2016 election the most corrupt in the
nations' history. The Clinton machine even used
Facebook files of citizen's emails in their attempt
to beat Trump. The FBI spying on Trump's office
was illegal, and the first time in the history of
presidential elections that government agencies

attempted to fix an election. The CIA was also involved in the fix when key officials were involved in the Russia dossier, and the spying on Trump. John Brennan, the Director of the CIA, was fired when he lied to Congress about the CIA actions during the 2016 election. Evidently, the directors of the intelligence agencies are liars. There was corruption in elections in the 1800s, but the 2016 election was even more corrupt.

The FBI and the CIA were deeply involved with illegal actions attempting to damage Trump, and help Hillary during the 2016 election. The deceit was kept secret during the election; while both the FBI and the CIA were guilty of criminal activities, their expertise in hiding blunders was amazing. The FBI Spygate and the CIA involvement with the fake Russia dossier were not made public until former employees reported the facts. The criminal activities of both agencies were of course unsavory, but they were also illegal, and those guilty should be prosecuted. As the illicit FBI actions are uncovered, the public opinion of the FBI and the CIA has reached the lowest level in history.

The FBI hid the spying by claiming it was classified material, and it wasn't until a retired FBI agent reported the illegal spy work in 2017. Congress started an investigation, and when complete, the nation will be even more disgusted with the FBI.

The CIA Director went out quietly, and the CIA has dodged most of the criticism, probably because of the huge number of investigations going on in Washington. After the election, the criminal infractions came popping out of the woodwork. If Hillary had been elected, none of the offenses would have been exposed, and the Clinton Teflon would have worked again.

The Watergate scandal of the 1970s involving Nixon spying on the Democratic campaign was reported to be the worst political scandal in history, but the FBI spying on the Republican campaign office in 2016 was illegal and topped Watergate.

Hillary invented the Russia-Trump dossier by paying $12.4 million to Fusion GPS, a dirt-gathering firm, to write a document on Trump connections with Russia. The 32-page dossier was immediately proven false when the accusations were checked, but Democrats and the media jihad continued to accuse Trump of collusion with Russia.

The Russia-Trump issue became the main topic in the election despite the dossier being a fabrication. The media jihad made the Russia matter daily fake news throughout the election, and the Russia attack on the President continued in 2017 and 2018. Despite the lack of any evidence that Trump was involved with Russia, the media jihad made the Trump-Russia theme the main topic during, and after, the election.

Hillary's Russia Dossier

The dossier consisted of 17 memos written between June and December 2016, and was strictly a paid political attack on Hillary's political opponent. Voters see these types of political ads often during an election, but never in history has a political attack prompted an FBI Spygate, and a Special Counsel investigation of a president.

However, the voters paid no attention to the dossier or the Hillary designed Trump-Russia connection. A 2018 poll indicated that over 90% of the public believed the dossier to be false.

FBI Director Comey, the Trump hater, immediately started a major FBI investigation of Donald Trump. There were 173 FBI agents working against Trump in the investigation. The two years of FBI investigations found no evidence of any Trump connection with Russia, and a yearlong inquiry by the Special Council found no Trump collusion with Russia.

Special Counsel Mueller indicted several Russians for interfering in the election, but Putin claimed the individuals were actually not Russians. Mueller's indictment was a sham; the Russians would never be forced to come to an American court. It was only an effort to give the media jihad something for their fake news.

Putin also admitted that Russia has no way of influencing a U.S. election because the voting is decentralized and not part of the internet. The media and Democrats ignore this minor point. Russia did hack into the DNC in an effort to disrupt the politics of the election, but this had no effect on the election.

The entire Russia matter is fake news, the reporting of counterfeit misinformation. The media is excellent at sending out bogus reports with no accountability. It is truly astounding that a totally false document prepared as a political attack on Donald Trump became the most important topic of the 2016 election.

The FBI investigation of the 30,000 emails destroyed by Hillary *after the emails were subpoenaed* by Congress, showed the bias in the agency. FBI Director Comey was in charge of the investigation, and made the decision that Hillary was not to be indicted because she was the Democrat nominee for president. It was discovered in 2017 that Comey actually drafted a statement clearing Hillary *before* the email investigation was completed. Hillary even destroyed her email server and cell phones during the so-called *investigation.*

After Hillary deleted 30,000 emails AFTER Congress had subpoenaed the documents, the FBI began an investigation, but the entire inquiry was a sham. Comey called a press conference on July 5, 2016 to give the results of the FBI investigation.

Comey stated that Hillary was *extremely careless* in handling classified material; the original term was *grossly negligent.* The FBI also found that over a hundred emails contained classified material, and she lied about it. Despite these crimes, Comey stated that in his opinion, Hillary did not *intentionally* violate the law, and no charges would be filed. He said: *No reasonable prosecutor would take such a case.*

Comey was the *investigator;* only the Justice Department could make that decision. He went beyond his authority with his personal opinion, and was highly criticized by legal experts.

The flawed Comey investigation of the Clinton emails and the Russian collusion in the election caused President Trump to dismiss him as the FBI Director on May 9, 2017. Comey was also accused of *grandstanding and politicizing* the investigations.

Democrats criticized the firing of Comey, but the criticism was generally accepted to be politics. Comey had few friends, even in the Democrat community. Legal experts agreed with President Trump's actions, and reported that President Obama should have fired Comey after the infamous July 5, 2016 press conference.

Comey did not go out quietly. He continued his attacks on President Trump and claimed he was a political scapegoat. He lost most of his followers, and Congress started an investigation into his illegal actions during the election.

The interference in the 2016 election by the FBI was illegal, and caused the public respect for the top police agency in the country to fall to the lowest level in history. The corruption of the two premier intelligence agencies in the election was a first, and both agencies require a complete reorganization.

CHAPTER TWO

The Electoral College receives attention every four years, but most Americans know little about the system used to elect the president, or that the process was established in the Constitution. The losers who want to eliminate the electoral method should be aware that an amendment to the Constitution is necessary, and requires a two/thirds majority of Congress for approval.

There are 538 electoral votes so the magic number is 270 for election. Donald Trump won 304 electoral votes to Hillary Clinton's 227, and moved into the White House. Seven Electoral College delegates voted independently: Collin Powell received three votes, John Kasich one, Ron Paul one, Bernie Sanders one, and the *Faith Spotted Eagle,* received one vote. Those delegates made a joke of the election process.

Hillary won the popular vote, but the margin came from California, the state that had passed a law (UB 60) allowing illegals to vote. Trump would have won the popular vote if the illegal voters had not been allowed to vote.

Hillary wrote a book *What Happened* that covers the election, and clearly stated that she should be president since she won the popular vote. Al Gore also claimed he won in 2000 when he lost the electoral vote.

There have been five presidential candidates who won the popular vote, but lost the election. In addition to Hillary and Gore, Andrew Jackson, Samuel Tilden, and Grover Cleveland won the popular vote, but lost the electoral vote. Jackson and Cleveland were later elected president, winning both the electoral and popular votes.

Hillary says *I would have made a damn good president,* but voters strongly disagreed. The media also takes a shot at Trump when the Electoral College is mentioned, but it is like watching yesterday's news since the press had been criticizing Donald Trump for three years.

Many Americans do not understand the Electoral College and the name contributes to the problem. The presidential voting system outlined in the Constitution is actually a *process,* and has nothing to do with a college. The electoral method for electing the President of the United States dates back to the birth of the nation, and is the law of the land.

The Continental Congress met in Philadelphia 230 years ago and established a set of principles for governing the new nation, and named the charter the Constitution of the United States.

The representatives debated for several months on the method for electing a president, and ultimately decided that it was necessary to have electoral delegates represent the people. The Founding Fathers were concerned that large states could decide an election, or a political group could force citizens to elect a dictator. They were determined that the people would pick a president.

Continental Congress 1787

The Constitution has Seven Articles, with each Article defining how the government is to be managed. Articles One, Two, and Three define the three branches of government, which are the legislative branch (Congress), executive branch (President), and judiciary branch (Supreme Court). Articles Four through Seven list the rights of citizens and the signees of the Constitution. After months of study, the electoral voting process for electing a president was included in the executive branch (Article Two).

If the popular vote were used, the large states could control the election, and the smaller states' votes would not count. In 1787, the state of Virginia had ten times more people than Georgia, and Virginia voters could carry any election. Today, the population of California is 65 times larger than Wyoming and Vermont.

To provide the states the ability to have a say in the presidential election, the Continental Congress gave each state the authority to appoint electoral delegates to represent the citizens of each state. The delegates were given the responsibility for electing each state's candidate for president. The system became known as the Electoral College, and while not perfect, it has worked for 230 years.

Each state has electoral votes equal to the number of senators (two for each state), plus one vote for every member of the House of Representatives.

The Constitution was approved by several states in 1789, but delegates were concerned that it gave excessive power to the three branches. The issue was debated for over two years, and James Madison, the fourth president, authored the *Bill of Rights* in 1791 that included the first ten Amendments to the Constitution.

The Bill of Rights added restrictions for the three branches of government, and listed the personal freedom and rights of the people.

The First Amendment protects the freedom of religion, speech, and freedom of the press. The Second Amendment protects the right to keep and bear arms.

The attacks on the electoral system are assaults on the Constitution that is the supreme law of the land. Both Clinton and Gore used the Electoral College as their excuse for losing the election, while ignoring that the Constitution dictates that the electoral vote is the method of election. Both ignore the Constitution when claiming they should have been elected.

After years of pursuing her favorite dream, Hillary lost the 2016 presidential election because of her baggage and lack of a campaign strategy that included change. Her idea that the economy was not a problem showed her lack of empathy for those out of work, and proved that she was not close to voters. Instead of visiting areas with high unemployment and listening to the voters, Hillary was flying over these areas on her way to Wall Street.

The voters certainly recognized the economy was a problem with nine million unemployed, and forty-eight million people on food stamps. Both were record setting numbers. Hilary and the DNC evidently believed the Obama rhetoric that the economy was great, but all economic indicators were negative. The public knew the economy was a disaster, and voted accordingly.

The media bias and the crazy polls convinced Hillary and the DNC that she would win. Trump refused to believe the polls, and was constantly at odds with the press because of the media jihad. The reason for the bias against Donald Trump is a mystery, but the media attacked him right from the beginning. The media animosity and hate go beyond definition and reason; no other political candidate has ever received such criticism.

The hate against Abraham Lincoln in the 1860s was terrible, but not as bad as the venom against Donald Trump today. While Lincoln took the media attacks in silence, Trump fights back. His *fake news* onslaught against the media was successful in gaining public attention to the false press statements, and many voters ignored the media jihad against Trump.

The Clinton machine dominated the election. When Bernie Sanders became a threat to her winning the Democratic nomination, Hillary took over the DNC and cut off Bernie's funding. This illegal move forced Sanders out of the race, and discouraged Joe Biden from entering the contest. The DNC hid the Clinton takeover; the Clinton-DNC joint venture did not become public knowledge until 2018, when Donna Brazile, former interim chair of the DNC released her book, *Hacks.* Taking over the DNC was a major factor in Hillary obtaining the Democratic nomination. Evidently, the entire Democratic Party had decided Hillary was to be the nominee.

The Clinton machine also pulled a similar stunt against Republican Donald Trump with the dossier. The Clintons have a history of taking care of threats, often with unscrupulous actions.

Hillary and the Clinton-controlled DNC paid $12.4 million to Fusion GPS, a dirt-gathering outfit, to go after Donald Trump. Fusion hired Christopher Steele, a former British agent who earlier worked in Russia, to develop the Russia-Trump dossier.

According to emails that surfaced in 2018, Hillary fed accusations to Steele, and he used the data to build up the fake news dossier. Steele was also a Trump hater, and his dossier was full of holes and falsehoods. A simple check of the facts in Steele's documents revealed that the individuals were not in the locations mentioned in the dossier, and they denied the accusation. The dossier was obviously a fabrication, but the FBI started an investigation against Trump.

The Steele 32-page document, in spite of being false, became the main FBI tool. The agency used the dossier to obtain warrants to spy on Trump's campaign office. The warrants were issued by the FISA court, and were illegal since FISA is only for foreign surveillance.

The FBI attempt to spy on Trump's campaign office was worse than Watergate, and Congress began a congressional oversight review in 2018. The review uncovered documents that exposed the illegal FBI attempt to fix the election.

Donald Trump said many times that the election was *rigged,* and he was right. The FBI and DOJ used illegal tactics in the attempt to damage Trump. The FBI also used the fake news dossier to appoint the Special Council inquiry of President Trump, even though there was absolutely no evidence of any Trump collusion with Russia.

The government fix was in process, but Hillary's baggage was a major problem. While the email scandal and Benghazi were always on the table, her inability to handle the veracity issue was a major voter problem. Polls indicated 70% of the nation believed Hillary to be a liar. The lack of truthfulness problem hurt Hillary in both the 2008 and 2016 elections.

The lack of veracity issue was a deep-seated problem for Hillary. New York Times columnist William Safire called Hillary a congenital liar. The email scandal added to the veracity problem because using a private server as secretary of state indicated that she wanted to hide all her emails. You do not *accidently* go out of your way to avoid using the prescribed government system for handling emails, and her *right wing conspiracy* excuses were ridiculous.

At the Trump rallies, women dressed as convicts walked the aisles with a ball and chain, and the audience would yell *jail Hillary.* The email scandal kept growing despite Hillary claiming the issue was resolved; it was the highlight of the daily news. Hillary was never able to shed her baggage, and the lack of truthfulness was her big problem.

Hillary's baggage started in Arkansas with the Whitewater scandal in 1978, and continued throughout her political life. Opponents always claim that Hillary should be in jail.

The division between the two political parties in 2016 was the worst in history. In 1796, George Washington wrote a 32-page farewell address criticizing the political party system as being dangerous for the country, and he was right.

Alexander Hamilton started the political party chaos in 1790 when he formed the Federalist Party. Hamilton was a politician and was interested in increasing his political power. His views of government were similar to today's Democrat Party – large central government, high government spending, and a liberal view of the Constitution. Thomas Jefferson, Washington's secretary of state, objected to Hamilton's liberal ideas, and formed the Democratic-Republican Party in 1792 to oppose the Federalist Party.

The Federalist Party dissolved in 1824, and the Democrat and Republican Parties split. The Jefferson Republican Party continued with small government and a strict interpretation of the Constitution, and the Republican Party has maintained these policies through the years. The concept of small versus large government, and adherence to the Constitution are still the main differences between the two parties today.

The Democrat and Republican Parties' racism issue has changed over the years. Republicans adopted an anti-slavery policy in 1854, when slavery was accepted in the nation. The anti-slavery protocol has been the Republican policy throughout the past 163 years. The Democrat Party was always racist until the 1960s.

The original Electoral College system only provided voting for the president. The person winning the majority of the electoral votes would be elected president, but there was no vote for vice president; the runner-up would be the vice president.

Unfortunately, politicians did not read George Washington's farewell address because the political parties took control of the elections. Since there was no vote for the vice president, each party attempted to gain both the president and vice president offices. Both parties added candidates to the ballots to prevent the other party from winning the vice presidency. There were eleven presidential candidates in 1796 compared to one in 1788 and 1792. George Washington was the only nominee for president in the first two elections.

The political party organizations started a party-control effort immediately. Washington's warning about the political party system being damaging for the nation in his farewell letter was right on; however, the politicians of 1796 were more interested in gaining power than the good of the nation. This concept continues today.

The peaceful, dignified first election quickly changed to the power domination by the political parties. The power-grab attempt by both parties continues to this day, and the drive is so strong that character assassination and personal attacks are common during the campaign. The 2016 election was a perfect example of the vile conduct.

The Electoral College appeared to work well during the first two elections because George Washington was elected by a unanimous vote.

The flaw in the electoral system that omitted the vote for a vice president was an error that became a problem in the third election of 1796 when the president and vice president were in different political parties. John Adams of the Federalist Party was elected President, and Thomas Jefferson of the Democrat-Republican Party was the runner-up in the electoral voting, and was elected vice president.

As would be expected, the difference in political parties caused problems throughout John Adams' four-year first term. The failure to vote for the vice president position also caused a problem in the next election.

The first and only tie vote for president occurred in 1800. Thomas Jefferson and Aaron Burr tied with 73 electoral votes; the electors voted for both believing that Burr would be second in the voting and become vice president. John Adams, the incumbent, only won 65 votes, and lost. The House of Representatives decided the election. The voting in the House continued to the 36th ballot when Jefferson was elected president. The lack of a vote for vice president remained a problem until Congress passed the Twelfth Amendment to the Constitution in 1804.

70

Burr's chances for victory were damaged by Alexander Hamilton's efforts to defame his candidacy. Hamilton wrote letters to delegates claiming that Burr was too dangerous to be president. Hamilton's character assassination of Burr was similar to the Hillary claims in 2016 that the Russia dossier proved that Donald Trump should not be president. The facts did not prove either Hamilton or Hillary's arguments, but times were tougher in the 1800s; duels were used in the 1800s to resolve personal differences.

Hamilton also prevented Burr's election as governor of New York in 1804 with the same personal attacks, and this was just too much for Burr. Aaron Burr challenged Alexander Hamilton to the most famous duel in the nation's history in 1804. Hamilton had gone too far with his political attacks on his rival, and he was forced to accept the duel to save his honor.

Hillary's attempt to damage Trump's character during the 2016 election was similar to Hamilton's character assassination of Burr, but fortunately dueling had gone out of style.

Dueling was against the law in 1804, but New Jersey was lax in enforcing the dueling ban. The Burr-Hamilton duel was held July 11, 1804 in

New Jersey and Alexander Hamilton was killed. The person on the U.S. ten dollar bill did not live to be 48 years old. Hamilton's pistol shot missed Burr, but Burr hit Hamilton in the right hip. The large ball caused damage to internal organs, and lodged in his spine. Hamilton died the next day at age 47, and his behind-the-scene politicking days were over. A sad caveat: Phillip Hamilton, his oldest son, was also killed in a duel three years before his father's death. Phillip was only nineteen years old.

Alexander Hamilton started the political party system shortly after George Washington was elected in 1788, but his continuous efforts to tilt elections cost him his life. His Federalist Party lost power during the Jefferson presidency (1801-1809), and was dissolved in the 1820s, but Hamilton's liberal policies continued with the Democrat Party. The Democratic-Republican Party split into the Democrat and Republican parties, with the Democrats maintaining Hamilton's principles of liberalism and big government. The Republicans adopted Jefferson's policies of small government and conservatism. The principles of the two parties have remained constant over the years.

The political party battles continued, and the 1824 presidential election was one of the worst. Andrew Jackson won more electoral and popular votes than John Quincy Adams, but failed to win a majority, and the election went to the House of Representatives for resolution under the Twelfth Amendment to the Constitution.

Henry Clay, the Speaker of the House, was also a candidate for president but had no chance of winning. Clay used his influence to elect John Quincy Adams president. Adams promised Clay the secretary of state position if Clay would swing the election to Adams. Clay pressured House members to vote for John Quincy Adams and he was elected president on the first House ballot.

The political scene in Washington in the 1820s was corrupt, but the 2016 arena was even worse. Hillary's illegal takeover of the DNC eliminated Bernie Sanders from the race, and the FBI used the dossier to spy on Trump's campaign office. This was worse than the Watergate scandal of the 1970s that forced Nixon to resign the presidency. The FBI hid the Spygate scandal during the election, but a disgruntled FBI agent exposed the illegal spying in 2017.

While the 1824 election was rigged with the Adams-Clay subterfuge, it was simply dirty politics. The Clinton-FBI attempt to control the 2016 election was against the law. The FBI spying on Trump's campaign office was illegal.

Hillary's platform in 2016 was simply anti-Trump, while the Republican candidate Donald Trump outlined an extensive program for change. The majority of the voting public was demanding a change in government in the 2016 election, but Hillary failed to understand that voters were fed up with Obama's presidency.

One of President Trump's campaign commitments was to *Make America Safe Again.* The Immigration Office does not have an adequate vetting process to assure that immigrants are not terrorists, and the silent majority agreed with Donald Trump's plan.

Senator John McCain, a Trump hater, led the religious freedom argument that open borders were acceptable. The religion stance had no validity since the immigrants were not U.S. citizens. The Founding Fathers demanded religious freedom for our citizens, but foreign aliens who are not citizens of the United States are not covered in the Constitution.

McCain is the senior senator for Arizona, and the state bordering Mexico has a problem with illegal immigrants. He was so anti-Trump that he ignored the citizens of Arizona with his decision on the religious freedom argument.

The electoral system is always criticized when a candidate wins the popular vote and loses the electoral vote, but the *naysayers* who defile the Electoral College ignore the Constitution. The Constitution dictates that the Electoral College is the method for electing a president and is the supreme law of the land. Constitutional law is never discussed when the losing candidate and the losing political party objects to the Electoral College.

The Founding Fathers took considerable time developing the principles for running the new government; the Continental Congress met from February until the middle of September 1787 developing the Constitution. The delegates decided against a monarchy as the governing body, and chose a republic to govern the new nation. The Continental Congress was firm that the people would elect the president, and selected the electoral delegates to represent the citizens of each state.

Voting Booths

The Electoral College was developed by the Continental Congress to assure that all citizens could vote. To avoid collusion, the Founding Fathers decided that each state should elect delegates to represent the state's citizens. The Founding Fathers were concerned that a foreign country could influence elections, and force people to vote for a dictator. The Electoral College was designed to prevent this from happening.

California, with its large population, could decide an election if the popular vote was used instead of the electoral vote. Since California allows illegal immigrants to vote, non-citizens could very well decide the election if the popular vote were used to elect a president. The Founding Fathers had the foresight to avoid this problem.

CHAPTER THREE
THE PRIMARIES

Candidates for President in 2016

The primaries are confusing for most Americans, and the process seems to go on forever. The number of presidential candidates in 2016 was the largest group ever; it appeared that everybody wanted to be president. Those pictured above are only the semi-finalists; there were 562 candidates if the write-in candidates are included.

The number of candidates for president was ridiculous, and of course, most did not belong in the race. The write-in candidates had little or no chance of election, and probably just wanted to tell their grandchildren they ran for president. The twenty-two Democrat and Republican candidates was still a large number. The primaries sorted out the twenty-two until the conventions selected the final two nominees to run for election – Hillary Clinton and Donald Trump.

What are primaries? Are primaries included in the election process in the Constitution? How did they start? These questions need answers because most Americans do not understand the primary system, and most voters dread the six-month primary period. Eyes get hazy whenever the primaries are mentioned.

The nation's early elections involved unscrupulous actions by some politicians and by the mid-1800s political machines controlled elections. Tammany Hall was the leading machine, and paid voters to vote for the Tammany candidates. The corruption in elections became so dominant that several states bonded together to improve the election process.

Florida was the first state to develop a primary convention to select the state's candidate for president. Unfortunately, the convention was more of a social event than an organized political conference.

The 1901 Florida primary failed to correct the corruption problem when the Democratic Party Chairman eliminated the favorites, and selected the party candidate. Despite the Florida problems, twenty-two other states started using primary conventions to select their state candidate. The party machines had created such a problem that the states developed the primaries for electing presidential candidates.

Primaries are state-run conventions in which each state selects their candidate for president. Primaries are not mentioned in the Constitution; there were no political parties at the time the charter was written. The political parties created such divisive competition in presidential elections that a different method for sorting candidates was necessary, and the primary system became the method for selecting candidates. No other country uses the primary system and the people do not select presidential candidates in many countries.

The first two elections in the new United States were refined events. George Washington did not even campaign for office This was before political parties were in power. The parties create such power aggression that presidential elections today are *killer take all* affairs involving character assassination and underhanded tactics.

The political party system was developed soon after Washington was elected for his first term in 1788. Alexander Hamilton started the Federalist Party in 1790, and Thomas Jefferson countered with the Democrat-Republican Party in 1792. The Federalist Party policies were large central government with high taxes, while Jefferson's party believed in small government and low taxes. The Federalist Party fell out of power in 1824, and the Democratic-Republican Party split into two parties, Democrats and Republicans.

The Democrats remained with Hamilton's idea of large government, and Republicans took the small central government plan. The push for power by both parties created a dog-eat-dog conflict that continues to this day.

George Washington was against the party system, and predicted that the parties would destroy the election system, and he was right.

All 50 states, plus six territories, use the primary system. Primaries may sound simple, but the complexities of the system make it difficult to understand. State primary elections begin in late January or early February of each election year, and continue until June. Some states use a caucus, and others use a basic primary to select candidates.

The difference between a caucus and a primary adds to the confusion. The caucus system includes meetings discussing candidates before the delegates vote; in a primary, voters simply check a box to vote. There were 17 caucuses and 39 primaries in the 2016 election.

In addition to the caucus and primary voting differences, there are four types of primaries; open, partially open, closed, and partially closed. In a closed primary, a registered voter must vote only for the party with which he/she is affiliated. In the open primary, the voter may vote for any party candidate.

The differences in primaries vary from state to state, and this adds to the difficulty in understanding the system. Another confusing element is the method of awarding the electoral votes. Some states use a winner-take-all method of allocating electoral votes, while other states use a proportional method. Most Americans have trouble understanding why the states can't agree on one method of allocating the votes.

A further complication is that the two parties use different methods for awarding electoral votes. The Republican Party allows each state to determine the allocation – either winner-take-all, or the proportional method. The Democrats use the proportional method. The media never explains the intricacies of the primaries, and the voters are unable to understand the variations in the process, and simply accept the results.

The six-month period seems to last forever, but candidates add to the lengthy timing by starting their campaigns years before the election. Hillary began her 2016 presidential run immediately after leaving the secretary of state position in 2013, so her campaign actually lasted three years.

The confusion and lack of understanding make the primary system a costly, drawn-out process. The six-month timing should be shortened, and the cost should certainly be reduced. When the primaries started in 1901, the cost was minor, but over the years, the cost has become enormous; the primaries cost $0.5 billion in 2016. The primary cost was double the 2012 cost, and the total election cost was $7 billion compared to $4 billion in 2012.

The cost of the election was ridiculous; Hillary spent over twice as much as Trump with $1.3 billion to his $0.6 billion. Trump spent $66 million of his own money, but Hillary failed to contribute to her campaign costs. Wall Street contributed $2 billion to Hillary's campaign, almost one third of the total election cost. Trump refused contributions from Wall Street lobbyists.

Wall Street uses *return on investment* as their primary performance measurement. Surely, Wall Street moguls expected a big payback from Hillary in return for their $2 billion investment.

The primaries were designed to eliminate corruption, but the 2016 election was one of the most dishonorable in history with the Democrats and the FBI using illegal tactics. The *New York Times,* the Trump hating newspaper, reported that the Trump campaign contacted Russian agents during the primaries to defeat his opponents. There was absolutely no evidence of any Trump-Russia connection, and the article ignored the Hillary Clinton collusion with Russia. The *Times* is one of the prime anti-Trump media outlets. Research has shown that 94% of the *Times* articles on the primaries and election were anti-Trump.

Hillary started the Russia issue when she paid $12.4 million to Fusion GPS during the primaries to fabricate a story claiming Donald Trump was working with Russia to win the election.

Hillary was also involved with Russia when she was secretary of state. She approved the Russia owned Uranium One acquisition of a U.S. uranium firm in 2010. The CEO of Uranium One donated $145 million to the Clinton Foundation, and it was reported to be a *pay-for-play* deal.

The interesting fact about Hillary's claim that Trump was colluding with Russia, is that Hillary was actually the candidate involved with Russia.

The timing of Hillary's contract with Fusion was hidden in the woodwork, but the first payment was made in the spring of 2016. Trump was not yet the Republican nominee, but he appeared to be the leading candidate. The first Fusion dirt-digging work was not finished until June of 2016, so the Russia issue was not a key part of the primaries.

Peter Schweizer's book *Clinton Cash* became available in June 2016, and one chapter included the details of Uranium One. The book is a summary of all the foreign nations' *donations* to Bill and Hillary Clinton. The Clintons had millions of unpaid legal bills when Bill Clinton left the White House in 2001, but somehow the debts were paid. The media never pursued the issue because the Clintons were the media darlings.

Donald Trump accused Hillary of being involved with Russia in the Uranium One fiasco in a June 17 speech, but the media and the Clintons ignored the issue. Hillary used the right wing conspiracy excuse again.

The result of the Fusion contract was a 32-page document called the *dossier,* and accused Trump of colluding with Russia. However, when the dossier was checked for accuracy, the document was proven a fabrication. The Hillary funded dossier was the main issue during the election and post-election periods.

Despite the dossier being proven false, the media and Democrats treated it as manna from heaven, and constantly accused Trump of colluding with Russia. The fake news Russia-Trump issue became the main topic.

FROM
RUSSIA
WITH
LOVE

Hillary's Bogus Dossier

The entire Russia issue was a hoax. The Russia dossier was strictly a Democrat political dirt document paid for by Hillary to cultivate a Russia connection with Donald Trump. Former British intelligence agent Christopher Steele authored the dossier, but used fictitious meetings and episodes in the 32-page document. When journalists checked the meetings, they found that the individuals were in different locations when the alleged meetings took place.

The fake news dossier began with Hillary's political attack on Donald Trump, and it is amazing how a fabricated political accusation became the main topic of an election. Politics won over truthfulness.

The entire Russia-Trump accusation was fallacious, but Democrats and the media jihad kept it going throughout the election. The Russia-Trump parody will go down in history as the most ridiculous distortion of the truth in the 2016 election.

Hillary certainly created a monster with the Russia fraud, but it was discounted by most voters, and had little effect on the election. A poll showed that over 90% of voters believed the dossier to be false.

The primaries were certainly tainted with the Clinton and FBI actions, and the process seemed to go on forever. Even though seven of the twenty-two candidates dropped out of the race before the primaries, sorting out the remaining fifteen candidates seemed to take forever.

Hillary unofficially started her 2016 campaign in January 2001, and several other candidates started their presidential job search in 2014. The 2016 presidential process was longer than most since the media had selected Hillary as their candidate when she left the White House. Apparently, Hillary's presidential aspirations go back to her Arkansas days, but she lost to Obama in 2008 and to Donald Trump in 2016.

When Hillary left the secretary of state position in 2013, an ABC poll showed that she would be the favorite in 2016. However, the same poll showed identical results when she ran against Obama in 2008.

Bernie Sanders was not considered a top candidate, but he would soon prove otherwise. The other three Democratic candidates Martin O'Malley, Lincoln Chafee, and Jim Webb did not have a chance.

The Republican field was more crowded; there were seventeen capable candidates, although the media gave Donald Trump no chance of winning. The anti-Trump bias started early.

The Lincoln-Douglas meetings of the mid-1850s pioneered the process of candidates presenting their campaign promises in debates. The debates would be a long, drawn-out process in 2015 and 2016.

The first televised presidential debate was between John F. Kennedy and Richard Nixon in 1960, and the Kennedy debate victory led to his election. Nixon blamed the debates for his loss, and refused to debate in 1968 and 1972. The Ford-Carter debate in September 1976 was the first presidential debate in sixteen years.

The candidates dropping out of the race before the primaries started were Democrats Lincoln Chafee and Jim Webb; Martin O'Malley withdrew after the Iowa caucus in February 2016.

Five Republicans including Lindsey Graham, the Senator from South Carolina, George Pataki, former Governor of New York, Bobby Jindal, Governor of Louisiana, Scott Walker, Governor of Wisconsin, and Rick Perry, former Governor of Texas, dropped out of the race in late 2015.

Scott Walker was an early favorite, but his Wisconsin accomplishments did not get him enough votes to continue running; he withdrew from the race in September 2015. Rick Perry of Texas was also considered a favorite because of his work in Texas, but he also dropped out in September 2015. The short run by the early favorites was significant, and an indicator of things to come.

The 2016 presidential election year began with the Iowa caucus on February 1 and the New Hampshire primary on February 9, 2016. The first primaries are extremely important because they set the tone for the election. Some experts claim the Iowa and New Hampshire votes are five times more important than votes in later state primaries. The Iowa caucus is critical because it is the first, but the winner of the Iowa caucus has only won the presidency three times. The New Hampshire primary is considered a better indicator of the presidential election since the candidate winning the state was elected president in the 1952-1988 period.

Trump won the 2016 New Hampshire primary, and went on to win the Republican nomination. Bernie Sanders was a surprising winner in New Hampshire, and beat Hillary with a two-to-one margin. This was not only a shock for the media and the Hillary followers, but a definite sign that Hillary had a problem. Hillary's forty years of baggage was the problem.

There were twenty-four debates in the 2016 election; twelve Republican and eight Democrat primary debates, and four general election debates. The debates are always touted to be extremely important by the media, but this is expected since debates are a media show similar to the Oscars in Hollywood. The media indicate that the debates decide the election, but 86% of voters do no change their votes; the value of the debates is far less than the media reports.

The five Democrat candidates met in Las Vegas on October 13, 2015 for the first Democratic debate. Hillary, Bernie, Martin O'Malley, former governor of Maryland, Jim Webb, former Secretary of the Navy, and Lincoln Chafee, the governor of Rhode Island, were the Democrat contestants.

While Hillary was expected to win easily because of her debate experience, the results showed a Bernie Sanders win; Hillary had a problem. The other three candidates were obvious losers. Chafee and Webb withdrew from the race a short time later, and O'Malley dropped out after the Iowa caucus.

The Republican debates began August 6, 2015 in Cleveland with the Fox News debate. The debate became famous when Megyn Kelly, one of the Fox moderators, attacked Donald Trump for his comments about women. Trump responded *You don't like me very much,* which was an understatement. Kelly's repulsive attacks on Trump were overdone, and she left Fox a few months later.

There were four more Republican primary debates in 2015, and seven in 2016. The debate process continued until March 15, 2016 in Miami, and by that time 13 of the 17 Republican candidates had dropped out. The *final four* were Donald Trump, Ted Cruz, Marco Rubio, and John Kasich. Surprisingly the Miami debate was civil, and called a draw. Donald Trump took center stage in all Republican debates, and his media coverage topped the other candidates.

The Florida primary of March 15, 2016 was held the same day as the final debate, and with 29 electoral votes, the state was all-important. Florida's Senator Marco Rubio was the favorite to win but he only took 27% of the state votes, a disaster for Rubio. Donald Trump did it again, winning 46% of the Florida votes, and gained the 29 electoral votes. Cruz was a poor third with 17%, and Kasich took 6%.

After winning Florida, Trump claimed, *It's over.* Marco Rubio dropped out a week later; Cruz withdrew on May 3, and Kasich dropped out May 4. Donald Trump had kayoed all sixteen Republican candidates in the primaries. For a candidate who the mainstream media claimed had no chance of winning, Donald Trump won the Republican nomination and would go on the win the presidency. The media and Democrats obviously underestimated Donald Trump.

Donald Trump's victory in the primaries was his own doing. Trump defied the campaign-spending idiom that the winner of any election spends more than the loser. Jeb Bush, Ted Cruz, and Marco Rubio spent more money in the primaries than Trump, but failed to win the popular and electoral votes necessary to win.

REPUBLICAN PRIMARY SPENDING
$millions

Trump	Bush	Cruz	Rubio
$76	$138	$127	$112

REPUBLICAN PRIMARY RESULTS

Candidate	Primary Wins	Delegates Won	Popular Votes MM
Trump	41	1,725	14.0
Cruz	11	484	7.8
Bush	0	4	2.8
Rubio	3	166	3.5

Donald Trump won the primaries with 1,725 electoral votes, 488 more than the required 1237 to win. Ted Cruz finished a poor second; Rubio, Bush, and Kasich were not in the running.

The results of the primaries proved Donald Trump to be the big winner, and he was the top candidate for president. However, the other sixteen Republican candidates made up the best field the Republican Party had ever assembled. The group included senators, governors, business CEO Carly Fiorina, and neurosurgeon Ben Carson. The talent far outdistanced the Democrats.

The governors Jeb Bush, John Kasich, Chris Christie, and Scott Walker were mentioned as early favorites. Jeb Bush, the former Governor of Florida was picked to win the nomination by many pundits before the primaries, but his campaign never left the ground; he dropped out of the race in February 2016. His performance was surprisingly poor; the Bush name was evidently a hindrance rather than an asset.

The Bush family started an anti-Trump crusade, but the public ignored the *sour grapes* campaign, and the family that included two former presidents lost credibility. The Bush family obviously took Jeb's loss personally. Jeb Bush disappeared into the losers' morass.

The Democrat Party primaries took an unusual turn; a little-known senator from the small state of Vermont became a strong challenge to Hillary.

The Clintons, the DNC, and the media expected Hillary to sail through the primaries with little opposition, but Bernie Sanders won 40% of the Hillary-Bernie contests, and proved to be a threat to Hillary. Bernie Sanders is a Socialist, and his giveaway plan was working.

The Sanders' popularity was an indication that Hillary had serious problems with voters. His disapproval of the Obama's domestic and foreign policies was a key part of his attacks on Hillary. The Middle East disaster happened on her watch as secretary of state, and Bernie poured it on.

The strengths and weaknesses of the candidates were exposed in the primaries, and the debates emphasized the divergence. There were some surprises. Who would have expected Jeb Bush, the supposed gold-star Republican candidate, to lose to Donald Trump, the never-can-win candidate? In the Democrat Party, who would have expected Bernie Sanders, a little-known senator from the small state of Vermont, to beat Hillary in 40% of their contests?

The primaries allow the states to determine the presidential nominees. If any other system had been used, Trump and Sanders probably would have not been successful in the race.

Bernie Sanders was a surprisingly strong Democratic candidate. Hillary had serious problems with Bernie; even though she attempted to meet his giveaway programs, Bernie was always able to give away more than she could. The Clinton machine decided that something had to be done about the Bernie Sanders threat.

The Clinton campaign offered to *help* the DNC financially since the 2012 election had put the committee $25 million in debt. The Democrats had not been able to raise sufficient cash to pay off the debt, and were spending $4 million a month during the primaries.

Hillary's hidden agenda was to take over the DNC, and put her people in control of the committee. With control of the DNC, Hillary could stop funding the Bernie Sanders campaign, which would force Bernie to quit the race. Control of the DNC would also damage Joe Biden's chances of entering the race.

The DNC was disorganized, and agreed to the reorganization and takeover by the Clintons. Debbie Wasserman Schultz resigned, and Donna Brazile was named temporary chair of the Democratic National Committee.

Hillary immediately cut off DNC funding for Bernie's campaign, and he was forced to drop out of the race. There was probably some payoff to Bernie, because he went away quietly after nearly beating Hillary.

Bernie Sanders had financial problems; with three homes, and with a senators' salary of $174,000, he was unable to pay his credit card bills. Hillary probably slid some cash under the table, because Bernie paid off his credit cards, and his net worth increased to a million dollars.

Hillary Takeover of the DNC

In typical Clinton fashion, Hillary had *removed* her only remaining threat to the Democratic nomination. The ousting had required some illegal and underhanded tactics, but that was normal for the Clinton machine. The Democrat threat was disposed of, and Hillary was nominated at the Democrat Convention on July 28 in Philadelphia.

Donald Trump was voted the Republican nominee for president at the July 21 Republican convention in Cleveland. John Kasich, the disgruntled Governor of Ohio refused to attend the convention. Kasich finished a poor fifth in the primaries, and accumulated 4 million popular votes to Trump's 14 million. His ego prevented him from endorsing Trump, and Kasich retreated to the loser's basement offices. Kasich was a loser who deserved to lose.

Donald Trump and Hillary Clinton won the primary battles and the necessary delegate votes at their conventions to win the nomination. Hillary's trickery with the takeover of the DNC enabled her to beat Bernie Sanders, but Trump's win was above board.

The primary system is cumbersome and difficult to understand, but it works. The people in each state vote for their presidential candidate instead of the political machines that dominated elections in the 1800s. The small states are heard with their electoral votes, and the large states of California and New York are unable to control elections. No other country uses the primary method; their candidates are selected with little input from the general population.

Unfortunately, the 2016 primaries were corrupt with the Clinton takeover of the DNC, and FBI spying on Trump. The corruption was not exposed during the election, and the voters were unaware of the Clinton fraud and the illegal FBI spying on Donald Trump.

Fox News and One America News covered the FBI spying on Trump's campaign office, but the mainstream media ignored the atrocity. Watergate was in the news in the early 1970s, but the media jihad completely ignored the 2016 spy tactic by the FBI.

The reason for the difference is that Watergate involved Republicans, and Spygate involved Democrats. The ultra-liberal Democratic media went after Republicans with a vengeance in 1972, but left the Democrats alone in 2016.

The false dossier received all the media attention because of the media bias. How the Clinton $12.4 million dossier prepared by an unscrupulous firm, proven to be a fabrication, and included Hillary's attacks on Trump, could take over the election news is incredible. When historians write about the 2016 U.S. presidential election, Russia will be the main subject – which is unbelievable.

The mainstream media have also ignored the Hillary Clinton Uranium One pay-for-play operation, and this will be the second topic for historians. The $145 million *donation* to the Clinton Foundation by the CEO of the Russian firm Uranium One has never been explained. Bill Clinton also received $500,000 for a twenty-minute speech in Russia.

Hillary uses the right wing conspiracy excuse for giving 20% of U.S. uranium resources to Russia. The *New York Times* columnist William Safire's statement that *Hillary Clinton is a congenital liar* seems to apply to the Uranium One scandal.

The Clintons have avoided sex scandals, real estate (Whitewater) scandals, Benghazi scandal, and the all-time award winner, the email scandal. The Clinton Teflon had worked miracles from Arkansas to Washington, and still worked in 2010 with the Uranium One pay-for-play with Russia, and in 2016 with the Russia dossier that was paid for by the DNC and Hillary.

Hillary made it through the primaries by a whisker, but her Republican opponent in the election would be more imposing. Donald Trump was on a roll, and would be a real threat.

CHAPTER FOUR

ELECTION 2016

The 2016 election was the nation's 58th presidential election; one of the closest and most costly, and unfortunately the most corrupt. Donald Trump won 304 electoral votes to Hillary's 227 and moved into the White house.

Hillary won the popular vote with 2.1% more votes than Trump, but lost the election when she failed to win the electoral vote. While Hillary's popular vote margin has been widely publicized, the media have ignored the fact that Trump's 46% beat Bill Clinton's 43% popular vote margin in 1992.

Hillary complained that by winning the popular vote, she should have been elected president. However, she ignored that the margin came from California. The ultra-liberal state gave Hillary 4.2 million more votes than Trump; Hillary's margin over Trump in the national vote was 2.8 million.

The cost of the 2016 election was $6.5 billion – twice the cost of the 2012 election. Hillary spent twice as much as Trump, and as Will Rogers said: *Politics has got so expensive that it takes a lot of money to even lose.* Rogers also said *The only redeeming thing about an election is that it will soon be over.*

The first elections in America cost didn't cost anything. George Washington did not run for office; the Continental Congress convinced him to accept the nomination, and he was elected by a unanimous vote in 1788 and 1792.

Washington refused a third term because he tired of media criticism. Newspapers even criticized his military actions during the Revolutionary War. Evidently, media jihads against the president date back to George Washington days.

The political parties were formed during George Washington' first term, and he was strongly against the party system. When he retired in 1796, Washington wrote a 32-page *Farewell Address* to American citizens. His words *I fervently beseech the Almighty to avert or mitigate the evils they may tend.* Washington mentioned the evils of political parties and financial difficulties in not balancing the budget.

Politicians since the 1790s have ignored his warnings. The political party system has controlled elections for 228 years, and Congress has balanced the budget only five times in the past 60 years. George Washington's foresight was truly astounding.

The political party system changed the election process from the quiet, dignified elections of 1788 and 1792. Today's elections are too costly, and include vendettas and character assassination.

The division in parties soon led to graft in party machines. Political corruption of Tammany Hall controlled Democratic politics from the 1800s to the mid-1960s, but today's political party system picked up where the Hall left off. Tammany Hall was famous for eliminating candidates who were not part of their system, and the Democratic National Committee eliminated Bernie Sanders during the 2016 election. Bernie was not part of the system.

Hillary had taken over the DNC during the primaries and cut off funding for the Sanders campaign. The Donald Trump comment that the system was *rigged* was right on.

The nation's first two elections were uncontested, and demonstrated the culture of the Continental Congress. With the development of the political party system, the refinement disappeared. The politics include mudslinging, name-calling, and personal attacks. The political parties are involved with graft and corruption, and the government does absolutely nothing about it. Members of Congress are part of the political party system, and there is no way politicians will police themselves. Politicians are simply *politicians.*

The number of candidates for president in the 2016 election was the largest ever, with five Democrats and seventeen Republicans running for president. The Republican field was stronger, and included governors, senators, and two business CEOs; the Democrats were politicians with little business experience.

The election would turn into dog-eat-dog contest, very different from the refined elections of 1788 and 1792 when George Washington was elected. The change from George Washington's pious attitude to today's aggressive demeanor is almost sacrilegious. Times have changed; it appears that everybody wants to run for president despite the attack system created by the political parties.

The political atmosphere of elections is unappealing to the electorate, and some actually refuse to vote. However, in 2016 voters were so upset and angry with the government that a *movement* took hold, and many new voters decided to cast their ballots to change Washington. The attitude change by the public had been developing for several years but politicians had not paid attention. Democrats had been kicked out of office in 2010 and 2014.

When politicians make speeches about *helping the American public, voters* have learned to watch out because legislators care little about *American taxpayers.* Congress had failed to address the problems of high taxes, the national debt, the high cost of Obamacare, and unemployment; voters finally determined that politicians' only interest was reelection.

The Hillary fairy tale dossier about Trump-Russia collusion created worldwide attention to the Russia topic. Democrats and the media jihad have continued the Russia matter through 2017 and 2018.

Hillary and the media claimed that Trump had tampered with the election by working with Russia, but the Democrats actually were guilty of attempting to fix the 2016 election. Hillary had corrupted the Democratic primary with the takeover of the DNC, and the FBI Spygate on Trump's campaign office was illegal.

The top-level FBI people were working for Hillary; the first time in history that a government agency was involved in fixing a presidential election. FBI Director Comey and Deputy Director McCabe were fired for their involvement.

The 2016 election was the most corrupt in history. There was dishonesty in the 1800s, but it was nothing compared to the unscrupulous fraud of the FBI in 2016. Top FBI officials rigged the election and even put an FBI spy in the Trump campaign office, but the agency refused to cooperate with investigators.

A former FBI agent exposed the illegal FBI actions and Congress began investigations in 2017. The congressional inquiries continue in 2018, and a special investigator may be appointed to inspect the FBI.

The Clinton control of the DNC was hidden from the public and the media. It was not made public until 2017 when Donna Brazile, successor to Schultz, reported the takeover by the Clintons. Brazile was a Hillary supporter, and gave the questions to Hillary before the CNN debate.

However, after being named the chair of the Committee, she was appalled at the Clinton actions, and the rejection of Sanders. Evidently, Brazile was attempting to prove that she had nothing to do with the fraudulent work of the Committee when she authored her book *Hacks.* In addition to the criticism of the DNC, Brazile was extremely critical of Hillary Clinton.

Bernie Sanders proved to be a popular candidate with his *giveaway* program, and even though Hillary attempted to meet his freebies, she always came up short. Bernie won 40% of the Clinton-Sanders contests.

Hillary soon realized that Bernie was not going away, and the Clinton machine decided to do something to fix the Bernie Sanders threat. The Clintons took advantage of the DNC financial problems; the 2012 election costs remained unpaid and the DNC was in the red to the tune of $25 million. The committee was spending $4 million a month on the 2016 campaign, and was unable to pay the bills.

The Clinton machine offered to help with the finances if the DNC would agree to Hillary taking over the Democratic National Committee. The chair of the Committee, Debbie Wasserman Schultz, resigned and Donna Brazile took control. The DNC agreed to the takeover by the Clintons, and Hillary put her people in charge. The DNC cut off funding for Bernie's campaign and he soon quit the race.

The unprecedented takeover of the DNC by a candidate was not reported during the election; it was not until January 2018 that the unscrupulous takeover was uncovered. Donna Brazile criticized the Clinton actions in her book *Hacks,* and Brazile's book received little media attention, but exposed Hillary's tactics.

After disposing of Bernie Sanders and Joe Biden, Hillary was certain to be elected the Democratic nominee. However, Hillary's email scandal would not go away. The email fiasco should have eliminated her candidacy, but FBI Director Comey saved Hillary from prosecution.

The FBI investigation into the email issue uncovered over a hundred emails that included classified material. Hillary was guilty of mishandling classified material, which was a felony. Comey took upon himself to presume that Hillary did not *intentionally* commit the crime. He also presumed that *no reasonable prosecutor would take such a case.*

Comey exceeded his authority with this decision, and he was later fired for his actions. Instead of going to jail, Hillary was able to continue her effort of becoming the President of the United States. Congress is now investigating the email decision by Comey, but nothing will happen. The Clinton Teflon worked again. The *double standard rule* always applies to the Clintons.

The Clinton machine has been successful in dodging scandals since their days in Arkansas, and the email offense was just another charade.

After disposing of Bernie Sanders and Joe Biden, Hillary was on her way to becoming the Democratic nominee for president. However, Donald Trump was close to becoming the Republican nominee, and the Clinton machine needed a plan to discredit Trump.

Hillary decided to tie Trump to Russia to damage his chances in the election. The DNC and Hillary used an outside firm, Fusion GPS to develop a Russia-Trump connection. Bruce Ohr, a top official of the DOJ, recommended Fusion; his wife Nellie worked for Fusion. Hillary paid $12.4 million to GPS to develop a plan to tie Trump to Russia. Russia had threatened President Obama during the 2012 election, and Hillary believed the Russia issue would eliminate Trump.

The unscrupulous outfit hired Christopher Steele, a retired British agent who had worked in Russia, to create a 32-page document consisting of 17 memos. The papers were given the moniker the *dossier*. The dossier reported that Trump held meetings with Russian officials attempting to have Russia damage Hillary's campaign. The first of the memos was released on June 20, 2016, just in time for the election.

The dossier was a political narrative intended to damage Trump. However, when the dossier was scrutinized, the document was proven a fabrication. The individuals who supposedly met with Trump in Russia were in different locations when the fake meetings were held. The sources used by Steele were not identified, and the Russia-Trump dossier was immediately proven false.

The fake news dossier was so flawed that the media at first refused to accept the document. John McCain solved the media jihad problem. Known as a Trump hater, McCain sent an aide to London to get a complete copy of the dossier. He made copies for the FBI, and members of Congress. Surprisingly, the anti-Trump work by John McClain received little publicity.

Since McCain was a Republican and endorsed the fake dossier, and *BuzzFeed*, the social media firm, published the Russia-Trump dossier. FBI Director Comey passed a copy to a friend who gave it to the press. Comey also leaked the FBI dossier report to the media.

The FBI leak started a chain reaction that resulted in nuclear fusion against Donald Trump. The unprincipled media treated the Russia-Trump dossier as a godsend, and started attacking Trump on a daily basis. Trump accused *BuzzFeed* of publishing fake news to no avail.

The Russia accusations against Donald Trump heated up and Hillary continuously baited the media with Russia-Trump claims. The false dossier was the ammunition for the war against Trump with the Russia claim.

The Russia issue continued throughout the election, through the post-election period, and into 2018. The media jihad picked the dossier up like a grenade, and threw the incendiary into worldwide news. The media treated the Russia dossier as gospel, and made it front-page news despite the fact that it was a falsified document.

The Hillary funded Russia dossier will go down in history as the main issue in the 2016 election. How a false document controlled the election news and the government actions is truly amazing. The entire Russia matter is indicative of the power of the press. However, the voting public saw through the media attempt to destroy Donald Trump. Most considered the dossier *fake news,* and ignored the document. A recent poll showed that over 90% of Americans believe that the dossier is false, and the document had little effect on the election.

The Trump connection with Russia, no matter how fictitious, became the most important political issue in the election. Hillary used the Russia collusion in every debate. Russia became the key topic of the election, and continued because of the FBI and Special Counsel investigations. A political fairy tale became scripture in the 2016 election with the help of the media jihad.

Hillary and the $145 Million Donation

The Clinton machine was again successful in creating a false attack on a political opponent, but the Russia matter would be a serious problem for Hillary. Both Bill and Hillary were involved in a pay-for-play transaction with Russia when Hillary was secretary of state.

Hillary approved the Russian Nuclear Agency acquisition of the Canadian firm Uranium One in 2010. The firm owned 20% of a U.S. uranium mining company, so Russia gained control of U.S. uranium deposits with the acquisition. The CEO of Uranium One *donated* $145 million to the Clinton Foundation, and Bill Clinton received a $500,000 fee for a 20-minute speech in Russia.

A committee called CIFUS – the Committee on Foreign Investment in the United States, must approve any foreign investment in a U.S. company. The responsibility of CIFUS is to review the national security implications of any foreign investment in a U.S. firm. There are sixteen members of the CIFUS committee including most Cabinet members. Hillary, as secretary of state, was a member of CIFUS. President Obama also approved the Uranium One acquisition.

With national security at risk with the Russia Nuclear Agency obtaining 20% of U.S. uranium deposits, it was unusual that Hillary, top-level people in the administration, and President Obama would approve such a transaction. The approval of Russia obtaining the nation's uranium made no sense.

After CIFUS and President Obama approved the Uranium One acquisition, the FBI started an investigation. The State Department, under Hillary's direction, reported that the acquisition did not have any national security risk, and the investigation was canceled.

The national security risk was certainly an issue since uranium is the most important element in nuclear fusion, and America imports uranium. Why would the Obama administration approve giving 20% of the nation's supply of uranium to Russia? Hillary, as secretary of state, was the main influence in the approval process.

It was suspicious that the government kept the acquisition secret, and the media failed to report the Clinton-Russia involvement at the time. The Clinton actions in the Russia uranium deal were a pay-for-play operation by both Hillary and Bill Clinton. They were paid by the Russians to approve the Uranium One acquisition so Russia could obtain the U.S. mining firm that supplied 20% of the nation's uranium.

Hillary had indicated that she was *against* the Uranium One acquisition before the gifts from Russia. After the gifts, she voted for the acquisition. The Uranium One deal smelled.

The Uranium One approval was hidden by the government and did not receive attention until Peter Schweizer published his book *Clinton Cash* in July 2016. Schweizer's book uncovered several suspicious Clinton deals that paid millions to the Clintons. The Uranium One deal that paid $145 million to the Clinton Foundation was covered in detail, and exposed the Clinton play-for-pay operation.

Somehow, the Clintons were able to defuse the Schweizer book. The mainstream media certainly was not going to report the criminal activity of their favorite presidential candidate. Fox News briefly covered the payoff, but the issue simply died away and was not an election issue. The Clinton machine was able to dodge another damaging scandal.

It is surprising that the Hillary connection with Russia was not an issue during the primaries or the national election. The Uranium One acquisition had not received any attention by the media, but the Schweizer book exposed the Clinton guilt. Donald Trump covered the Hillary-Russia pay-for-play in the debates, but the moderators failed to get involved. The details should have been explosive in the debates.

Peter Schweizer did an excellent job with research, and his *Clinton Cash* exposed several foreign nation *donations* to the Clintons. When Bill Clinton left the White House in 2001, the Clintons were deeply in debt because of unpaid legal fees. The Monica Lewinsky trials cost millions. The debt mysteriously disappeared.

Instead of Donald Trump being involved with Russia as Hillary's dossier claimed, Russian agents paid off the Clintons in the Uranium One deal in 2010. The Clintons were actually guilty of dealing with Russia, but somehow they were successful in pushing the Russia ball into Donald Trump's court. The Clinton machine had an excellent system for dodging scandals, and they certainly switched the Russia connection from Hillary to Trump.

It is astounding that the Hillary connection with Russia was kept quiet during the election, particularly since the Schweizer book accurately reported the matter. The media jihad ignored the Clinton-Russia incident, and the conservative news channels failed to make an issue of the Hillary connection with Russia. The Hillary Russia involvement was swept under the rug, and never became an issue during the election.

The Russia-Trump issue started as a dirt –
gathering effort by Hillary against her political
opponent, but developed into worldwide news.
The Clintons must be laughing when they see
reporters chasing their Russian ghost attacking
Trump. Impeachment is even mentioned.

Despite the fabrications and falsehoods, the
dossier succeeded in giving the media jihad more
ammunition to be used against their mortal
enemy, Donald Trump. Although reasonable and
intelligent journalists would be expected to
verify their sources, these jihad people grabbled
the dossier and ran. ABC, CBS, CNN, and NBC
criticized Trump every day for his involvement
with Russia. The episode was ridiculous because
Hillary created the fable as a political tool against
Trump; she even supplied most the dirt on
Trump to Christopher Steele.

In addition to Comey sliding a copy of the
dossier to the media, he used the dossier to
obtain warrants to spy on Trump's campaign
office. The *Washington Post* used the Republican
Watergate scandal to oust President Nixon in
1972; Comey was spying on Trump, and planned
to use the media to oust Trump from the race in
2016 – an amazing similarity.

James Comey

Comey doctored up a request for a warrant using the dossier as proof, and obtained warrants from the FISA court. The FISA court only has authority to spy on foreign intelligence individuals, but the FBI was spying on the Trump campaign office.

Comey was a Hillary supporter and a Trump hater, so the illegality did not seem to bother the leader of the nation's top police force. The crime carries a prison sentence so he should have been concerned. The FBI interference in the 2016 election was an illegal act to destroy Donald Trump, and Congress, with oversight responsibility, began investigations in 2018.

What started as an underhanded attack on a political opponent, ended up being the tool for an illegal FBI intervention into the 2016 election.

During the debates, Donald Trump told the audience that his phones were tapped. Evidently, the FBI is good at hiding their faults, because the moderator knew nothing about it, and moved on to other topics.

The FBI, under the direction of the renegade James Comey, started an investigation into the supposed Russia-Trump collusion attempt, but was unable to find any Trump connection. The FBI conveniently failed to report this minor detail; there have been no FBI reports on the so-called investigation.

The media fake news specialists reported the dossier ad nauseam. The media jihad was relentless, and the rhetoric was nauseating. The dossier was just what they needed to fuel the fire against Trump, ignoring that the document was proven false.

The media failed to report that the dossier was paid for by Hillary, and that the FBI Spygate was illegal. The Russia issue continued throughout the election, and into 2017 and 2018. The Mueller Special Counsel also found no Trump connection with Russia, but indicted several Russians in 2018 for suspected interference in the 2016 election. Putin said they were not even Russians.

The fabricated fake news dossier was simply an attempt by Hillary to eliminate Trump. The document was proven a fabrication, but the FBI continued with investigations. Hillary still uses the so-called Trump collusion as the main reason for her loss. The Russia-Trump issue was a fairy tale, but accepted as gospel by the Democrats.

Democrats and the mainstream media used the falsified dossier as the instrument to continuously attack Donald Trump. It was like a giant tsunami. Neither reported that the dossier was a fake document that was started and paid for by Hillary Clinton. Their problem was that the dossier wave was overdone – the public did not believe it. The Russia dossier was intended to destroy Donald Trump, but voters turned the tables and elected him President.

Documents surfaced in 2018 that started a congressional investigation of FBI interference in the election. The mainstream media fails to cover the issue, but conservative media expose the illegal FBI involvement. *Fox News* and *One America News* revealed the individuals in the FBI attempt to fix the election, and several were reassigned to other departments. Comey and McCabe were fired.

With Bernie and Joe Biden out of the race, the dossier negative publicity on Donald Trump, and the FBI spying on Trump, Hillary and the DNC were confident the stage was set for Hillary's victory. The media continued to predict a Hillary win, and the polls were still showing double-digit leads for the sure-fire winner. However, the election results would be the ultimate shock.

The poll results were another issue; they were wrong. There were over a hundred polls with most reporting big margins for Hillary throughout the election. Some polls were showing 30 and 40 point leads for Hillary, a staggering blunder. The polling errors have never been explained, but the huge margins made Hillary and the DNC overconfident, and affected their strategy.

The polls had been showing large leads for Hillary since she announced she was running for president. The media used the poll results to send the message to the voting public that Hillary was a sure bet to win. Many people in the polling sample were influenced by the forecasts of a Hillary victory, and replied to the pollsters they would vote for Hillary. Hiding their real feelings had a major effect on the bizarre poll results.

The TRF poll avoided the *Hillary for sure* error by asking *how will your neighbor vote.* The individuals used the neighbor question to express their true feelings. The results of the TRF poll were more accurate than the other 100 polls.

Hillary hid her baggage right from the beginning, but failed to see that the voters knew about most of the scandals. She believed the Whitewater, Benghazi, and Monica Lewinsky scandals were forgotten, and ignored the Russia Uranium One fiasco, the deleted emails, and the takeover of the DNC. The DNC hid the Clinton takeover, so she avoided this wrongdoing during the election.

Even though she was successful in keeping her Russia connection out of the election, it was exposed later, and is currently under investigation. However, Hillary was successful in pushing Russia into Donald Trump's court, and this was another Clinton charade.

The Clinton machine was able to hide all these issues during the election, but Hillary's prior sins caught up to her. Hillary's baggage was a problem. Voters did not accept the *right wing conspiracy* excuse for her email and Benghazi scandals, and her lack of truthfulness was a serious problem. The DNC and media failed to recognize just how serious these problems were.

Hillary's lack of veracity was a problem that never went away; polls showed that voters believed her to be a liar. Hillary is a *congenital liar,* and the problem was hitting home.

The Benghazi tragedy continued to haunt Hillary. She continually claimed that the attack on the diplomatic compound in Benghazi, Libya was a *sudden uprising* caused by some video that nobody had ever seen. The September 11, 2012 attack was premediated, and the U.S. Libyan Ambassador Christopher Stevens and three other diplomatic agents lost their lives. President Obama, Hillary, and Susan Rice, the U.N. Ambassador, continued to claim the video caused the uprising, but the public never accepted the video excuse.

The Benghazi tragedy was called the *Battle of Benghazi,* and received considerable negative publicity. The tragedy occurred while Hillary was secretary of state, and she was criticized for refusing Stevens' request for added security. Hillary's attempt to protect President Obama's reputation caused the disaster.

President Obama had proclaimed victory in Libya shortly before the attack, and that ISIS was a *JV team.* ISIS was in fact stronger and taking more territory in the Middle East. The CIA had done a poor job of intelligence, and the *Battle of Benghazi* was a surprise.

The security had been reduced by Hillary to show that Benghazi was a safe area. Stevens made requests for more security, but Hillary demanded that security be reduced. She was attempting to support Obama's claim that he was winning the war, but the lack of security caused the debacle.

Benghazi Tragedy

The Benghazi tragedy occurred less than two months before the 2012 presidential election, and Obama did not want the Benghazi attack to hurt his reelection chances. His attempt to play down the attack that killed four Americans, including the Ambassador, was a self-serving political ploy that was disgraceful.

The CIA developed *talking points* that blamed the terrorist attack on some video that offended Muslims. Susan Rice appeared on all news channels telling the false video story. The continuous claims by Susan Rice that the video caused the Benghazi tragedy is similar to the reply by Shakespeare's Hamlet: *methinks the lady doth protest too much.*

President Obama and Hillary also appeared on TV giving the video hoax as the reason for the Battle of Benghazi. The effort by the Obama hierarchy on Benghazi was simply too much. Hillary's use of the video as justification for her lack of providing security did not convince the voters.

The lack of any military response to save Ambassador Stevens and his people was another embarrassment. With all the military in the Middle East, you would think some group could have taken action. Congress questioned military leaders in the hearings, but the generals were reluctant to give details. It was apparent that they wanted to keep their jobs.

The military disclosed that Hillary demanded that the rescue team that was later sent to Benghazi remove their armored vests because it would appear too aggressive. The idea that riot gear would offend terrorists was not only ridiculous, but a clear indication that Hillary was more concerned by appearances than the safety of her people.

Benghazi would not have happened if the secretary of state had done her job. Heavy security was required in the dangerous Benghazi area, and Hillary's demand that security forces be reduced to show that Obama was right, was absurd. The removal of security was another *appearance* issue; Hillary was attempting to support Obama's campaign speeches that his policies were winning the war. The Hillary actions were negligent and criminal; how she could face the victim's loved ones is difficult to understand.

The refusal of the requests by Ambassador Stevens for added security, and the demand that the Benghazi security detail be removed has never been explained. The State Department simply refuses to answer the questions by the Congressional oversight committee.

The lack of adequate security cleared the way for the attack, and the death of four Americans. Hillary's attempt to show that Benghazi was safe without security was a tragic mistake.

Hillary was playing politics by attempting to show that security was not required since the President had assured the nation that he was winning the war. President Obama's declaration that ISIS was the JV team was a joke.

Hillary was following the party line, but sadly, the political effort was a disaster, and four Americans were killed. How Benghazi could happen to the strongest nation in the world is a mystery that will never be resolved. The House investigation has been going on for five years but has not been able to find out exactly what happened because the State Department, the CIA, and the military, have refused to answer questions under the claim of *classified material.*

Hillary's actions during the Benghazi attack demonstrated her lack of ability to run the State Department. The organization must make tough decisions, and political correctness should not be considered in decisions. Hillary was playing the political game instead of doing her job as secretary of state.

Hillary's lack of compassion was shown in the 2013 Senate Foreign Relations meeting. When asked about the cause of the Benghazi attack, her reply was, *what difference, at this time, does it make?* She was photographed yelling this answer to Senator Ron Johnson's question, *Why don't you pick up the phone and call the survivors?*

What Difference Does It Make

The reply *at this time what difference does it make* when Hillary was asked to call the victim's families was a typical Hillary response, but the public was disgusted. The reply received considerable negative publicity, and the voters were upset with her lack of sensitivity. Hillary took the political path rather than protect her people.

Not only did Hillary literally cause the Benghazi attack by removing security, she failed to immediately request military action to save the lives of the Ambassador and his people.

Lack of veracity and character were issues with Hillary, but she failed to mention these problems in her book. Lack of truthfulness was a major issue with voters, but Hillary failed to accept this to be a problem.

A classic example of Hillary's lack of truthfulness was the Whitewater probe. The special counsel subpoenaed her payroll records from the Rose law firm in Arkansas during the investigation, but the records were never found. Payroll records are normally easy to find, but not in Hillary's case.

Surprisingly, nine years later, when Hillary was the first lady, she found the box of records in her White House quarters. The statute of limitations had expired a short time before she found the box in the White House. Hillary must have been walking around the evidence for nine years, but she claimed she *honestly didn't know* the box was filled with her subpoenaed records. Honesty is the key word in that assertion. Americans did not accept the excuse.

Lack of trust is a problem for most politicians since they often vacillate on political issues. People simply do not vote for candidates who are liars, and Hillary was no exception.

The bottom line is that Hillary was not electable because of her lack of integrity and truthfulness. These were certainly key voter issues, but Hillary and the DNC failed to recognize the problem.

Hillary was extremely cunning with the DNC takeover, and the Russian dossier against Donald Trump; the takeover enabled her to win the Democratic nomination, and the dossier became the main topic of the election.

The FBI was a willing ally, and used every underhanded tactic possible to undermine Donald Trump. Hillary and the Clinton machine were using every asset in Washington to help the election process. The FBI-Hillary joint venture was the first time in history that a government agency had interfered in a presidential election.

Donna Brazile, former interim chair of the DNC admitted that the DNC rigged the election in her book *Hacks.* Brazile even gave the debate questions to Hillary *before the debate,* a violation of debate rules and protocol.

Despite the illegal DNC and FBI activities, Hillary still lost the election. Voters obviously disagreed with her statement that *I would have made a damn good president.*

The elections in the 1800s were corrupt, but Hillary, the DNC, and the FBI, managed to make the 2016 election the most corrupt in American history. The media bias against Donald Trump was obvious with the media jihad, but the DNC and FBI fraud went unnoticed until after the election. The Clinton tricks were to be expected, but the FBI schemes were surprising.

The media fails to report the FBI tactics, and many Americans are unaware of the illegal activities. Die-hard Democrats ignored the Clinton and FBI suspicious actions, evidently believing the corrupt actions were typical Clinton politics. The Democratic Party and the media refused to accept that the FBI interference was illegal, and continued to claim that Trump was in collusion with Russia. The facts certainly prove otherwise.

With illegals voting in California and other states, the number of people voting Democratic continues to increase, and the party chiefs Chuck Schumer of New York and Nancy Pelosi of

California hold the government hostage over illegal immigrants. The Democrat tag team refused to approve a budget in 2017, and shut down the government on January 20, 2018 over immigration. Democrats demanded that illegal immigrants be allowed to vote.

Democrats pay no attention to immigration laws, and demand that illegals can vote. The obvious reason for this ridiculous demand is that illegals vote for Democrats, and the Democratic Party is attempting to gain more Democrat voters. They never admit to this plan, but most in the silent majority certainly recognize the scheme. The mainstream media follows along with the Democrat plan to allow illegals to vote. The Democrat actions of stopping the wall, and continue to allow illegals to enter ignores immigration law.

The Democrats are obviously more interested in gaining more Democratic voters with the illegals than protecting American citizens. The politics by the Democrats is against the law, but the media goes along with the ridiculous plan.

The Democrats also refused to approve a budget for four years during the Obama administration. Harry Reid, the Democrat

Senate Majority Leader was responsible for blocking the budget, but four years was ridiculous. One of the politicians' main jobs is to finance the country, and failing to approve a budget certainly proves the Democrats are more interested in party politics than doing their job as elected representatives of the people. There must be a better way to run a government.

Voters recognized the Washington problem, and have started their own jihad against the do-nothing politicians. The silent majority had started an effort to take their country back, with the mid-term elections during the Obama reign showing their anger. However, the pompous politicians failed to pay attention.

When the candidates were developing their campaign plans for the 2016 presidential election, most ignored the mid-term election results. Voters were angry; they wanted a change in Washington, and had rejected the incumbents in the mid-term elections. The majority of the voting public had changed their mindset on politics; they were tired of the weak politicians in Washington who failed to cut spending and balance the budget, and wanted new blood in Congress.

Hillary and the Democrats evidently paid little attention to the elections of 2010 and 2014, since both were continuing with the Obama weak economy, and his disastrous foreign policies. They should have been listening to the voters. Donald Trump was the only candidate to recognize that voters wanted a change in Washington.

Trump's *Make America Great Again* strategy included major changes; trade revisions to bring jobs back to the country, eliminating government business regulations, reducing taxes, correcting immigration problems, and draining the swamp. Voters liked his plan, and voted accordingly.

The proposed changes hit home with the silent majority, and draining the swamp agreed with their ideas. Trump's nationwide rallies saw thousands of blue-collar and white-collar workers sitting together. The rallies and his continual fight with the media made Trump a household name, and his *fake news* claims turned the public against the media.

Democrats made a huge mistake by ignoring the voter issues. The singular focus of attacking Trump was not enough to attract new voters. The DNC and Hillary never established a new platform strategy, failed to research voter opinion, and depended on the anti-Trump focus as their campaign plan. This campaign strategy error has not received much publicity, but was a serious mistake by Hillary and the DNC.

There were wide differences between the Democrats and the voters' ideas on the problems facing the country. According to the *Pew Research Center,* an independent and non-partisan study group, 75% of the silent majority believed terrorism to be the biggest threat facing the nation, while only 40% of Democrats believed terrorism to be a major problem. This is unbelievable with the number of terrorist attacks.

Over 80% of the silent majority voters believed immigration to be a serious problem, but only 20% of Clinton followers thought immigration was a problem.

There were other wide differences in the *PEW* findings, but the terrorism and immigration differences indicate how far apart voters were from the Hillary strategy. Most Americans assume that everybody in the country is concerned about terrorism, but evidently, this is not the case. Climate change was the major concern of two-thirds of Clinton followers, but was not a factor with the silent majority.

Evidently, the Democrats had convinced their followers that the economy was great since only 40% were concerned about jobs, while two-thirds of the silent majority considered jobs to be a high priority.

The wide differences in the Pew data was an indication of how far apart the two parties were on key issues. The 35-percentage point difference on terrorism is unbelievable; with almost daily terrorist killings of innocent people, and the individuals who believe climate change is more dangerous that terrorism are out to touch with reality.

The media did not cover the differences between the Clinton voters and the silent majority, and the subject was not discussed in the debates. Even though some media channels held round-table discussions after the debates, none covered the wide differences between the Clinton followers' beliefs and public opinion. The media ignoring public opinion was a major error, and made most of the post-debate summaries by journalists pointless.

The media completely missed the differences between Democrats and the voters. The Democratic idea that global warming is more important than terrorism goes beyond reasonable thinking. Hillary and the DNC evidently failed to do sufficient research into public opinion.

The debate moderators used the normal media issues of women voters for Hillary, and Trump's tweets. They failed to research the big differences between public opinion and the Democrat platform.

The failure of the media to research the voters' opinions before the debates led to the weak debate topics. The debate commentators appeared to be more interested in their TV appearance than the voter issues.

Donald Trump also had his problems; he was unable to keep a team together. The Trump campaign office was always in a state of flux, and the media jihad made this daily news. While his campaign team was changing, Donald Trump still maintained control. The changing Trump campaign office was always a media jihad topic, but Hillary was unable to take advantage of the situation.

Trump's first campaign manager, Corey Lewandowski resigned after accosting a reporter. Paul Manafort was next in line, but quit after five months because of an article about Manafort and the Ukraine. Less than three months before the election, Steve Bannon was appointed CEO of the Trump campaign, and Kellyanne Conway was made campaign manager.

The mainstream media criticized the changes at the top of the campaign organization, and continually predicted that Donald Trump had no chance of winning. The changes in the Trump campaign office, and his tweets about Hillary and Bill Clinton were receiving considerable negative publicity. Bannon and Conway were new on the job, and had a huge job to do in a short time.

Bannon used his attack method to go after Hillary, and the Clinton lead began to decline. However, a disaster occurred on October 7, 2016, a month before election night. The *Washington Post* reported a 2005 tape of Donald Trump bragging about sexual advances toward women. The media dubbed the tape P....gate and all TV channels covered the details repeatedly. The Trump tape was like manna from heaven for the media jihad.

Paul Ryan, the spineless Republican leader of the House, even declared that Trump should drop out of the race. The consensus of the media was that the tape was the final straw in Trump's campaign, and that there was no chance that he could survive the attack.

Donald Trump did not deny the tape, and explained that it was *locker room talk.* The media did not accept the excuse, and predicted that this was the end of the line for Donald Trump's presidential run. Hillary was even more vocal with criticism.

Steve Bannon was an experienced campaign fighter, but there were only twelve days before the third and final debate on October 19, 2016, and a month before the November 8, 2016 election. Trump was in deep trouble, but in typical Trump fashion, he decided to fight back.

The *Washington Post* held the Trump tape back until it would do the greatest damage and the plan was working. However, Trump decided to highlight Bill Clinton's rape accusations.

Ninety minutes before the third debate started, Trump held a press conference in Las Vegas with four Clinton accusers on stage. Trump's position was that he had said some stupid things, but Bill Clinton had actually attacked and raped women. The women supported Trump and attacked the Clintons.

The daily news changed from the Trump tapes to the Clinton rapes. The debate was nasty, but Donald Trump held his own, and the media reported a near tie. Even though Trump was successful in dodging the tape bullet in the debate, the subject was still a hot topic with the media.

The mainstream media released the Trump tape at the perfect time to affect voters on election night, but the Trump press conference countered the tape. Even the anti-Trump media coverage suddenly changed from the *Trump tape to Clinton rape.* The Bannon plan worked, and Trump remained in the race.

Trump continued the campaign trail with his rallies, but Hillary had slowed down. Some in the media even reported that she had health problems after the public saw her fall into a waiting SUV. She appeared weak, and needed help getting into the vehicle. The slowdown in campaign visits during the final weeks was unusual; Hillary made only 71 campaign stops, while Trump made 106, a 66% difference.

The third and final presidential debate was held in Las Vegas on October 19 2016. Chris Wallace of *Fox News* was the moderator. The debate was abrasive as expected, but most considered the debate a tie.

After months of debates, primaries, the Democrat, and Republican conventions, and daily battles between the candidates, Election Day was just around the corner.

The election period included several devious and illegal activities by Democrats, and made the 2016 election the most dishonorable in history. Hillary created the takeover of the DNC, the fake news Russia dossier, and her friends in the FBI attempted to fix the election.

The sudden withdrawal of Bernie Sanders was a shock for most, and was never explained, but the Democrat Party was set with Hillary as their candidate.

The media had named Hillary the winner for years, but the unknown senator from Vermont had put up a great battle. Bernie was a Socialist, but young Democrat voters liked him. It was necessary for the Clinton machine to take over the DNC and cut off funding for Bernie's campaign to force him out of the race.

The 2016 election will go down in history as the worst political fight in the 218 years of presidential elections. The Clintons, known to be dirty political infighters, took over the Democratic National Committee to force Hillary's chief opponent out of the race, and government agencies attempted to fix the election.

The FBI attempted to fix the election, and another agency, the DOJ was actively involved in bringing in a foreign agent, Christopher Steele, to fabricate a false dossier on Donald Trump. Both actions were illegal, and the FBI Director and his top aide were fired for their actions. The National Security Advisor was forced to retire after lying to Congress.

The government activities during the election were criminal, and Congress finally started investigations into the FBI and CIA actions. However, both agencies refused to submit data to Congress, and have been successful in blocking the congressional oversight committee investigations.

The government sins were hidden, and the voting public was unaware of the attempts to fix the election. The disclosure of the FBI and CIA interference in the election came from retired agents, and emails between other agents. The Justice Department appointed an investigator to look into the illegal FBI activities, but it is doubtful the agency can police itself. Based on the lack of FBI cooperation to date, it appears the agencies will continue to fight any effort to clean house and reorganize the corrupt agency.

The public lost confidence in the FBI, and once the sordid election details are exposed, there could very well be a public uprising. If Hillary had won the election, all the illegal actions would have been swept under the government rug.

Democrats have ignored the FBI interference in the election, and the mainstream media has never covered the issue. The FBI is good at hiding their mistakes under the cover of *classified information,* so the public is unaware of the illegal actions.

The final days of campaigning involved Trump visiting the rust-belt states of Wisconsin, Michigan, Ohio, and Pennsylvania. Hillary was evidently confident these Democratic states would vote for her. Trump won all four states by a small margin, and won the election. If Hillary had obtained just one percent more votes in each state, she would have won.

The election was held Tuesday November 8, 2016, and the polls were still predicting a Hillary victory. The following is the timeline.

· 9pm Indiana for Trump, Vermont for Hillary.
    · No surprise.

· 10:39pm Ohio declared for Trump.
    · Big shock for Democrats.

· 11:56pm Trump wins Utah and Iowa.
    · Another shock for Democrats – trend was for Trump.

· 1:35am Pennsylvania declared for Trump.
    · Pennsylvania's 20 electoral votes left Trump with 264 electoral votes, only 6 short of the magic 270.
    · Hillary was in a panic.

· 2:07am John Podesta, the Clinton campaign manager refused to concede.

· 2:33am Wisconsin is called for Trump.
    · The 10 electoral votes decide the election. Donald Trump was elected President

Donald Trump won the 2016 election despite the Clinton underhanded tricks, the FBI illegal spying tactics, and the media jihad against Trump. The silent majority had voted for their candidate because he was not a politician; they were tired of do-nothing politicians. Trump overcame the uphill battle with Washington and the mainstream media.

The *political experts* called Trump's victory the biggest upset in history, but it really was no upset. The voters simply decided he was the best of the twenty-two candidates for president. The Trump victory was a surprise because the negative polls and the media had been predicting a Hillary win for four years.

Clinton supporters were devastated. The media and the polls had been predicting that Hillary was to be the president and they simply could not believe the election results. The silent majority had taken care of business and elected Donald Trump.

Hillary had planned a big celebration party at the Javits Convention Center in Manhattan, and when the Trump victory was certain, John Podesta told the disheartened celebrators to go home. Many were seen crying as they pushed through the center's glass doors.

Hillary Clinton followers were heartbroken; after four years of constant media predictions, and poll results showing that Hillary was a sure winner, their world had caved in. The Democratic National Committee went into hiding; they had no answers.

The mainstream media could not believe the election results either. After criticizing Donald Trump for seventeen months, and using the Russia accusation throughout the election, Donald Trump was the 45th President of the United States. Hillary had lost a second time, and she could not understand it.

How could the candidate that the media had proclaimed to be not electable win the presidency? The results did not compute, but the media jihad and Democrats planned to discredit the president.

Hillary's golden carriage had turned into a pumpkin, and she had dropped the golden slipper. The *never can win candidate* had taken her rightful place as President of the United States. This was her second attempt for the presidency, and she lost both times.

Hillary's congratulatory phone call to Trump was hollow, and lasted less than a minute. She immediately continued with her foul language about the new president. Hillary also claimed that since she won the popular vote, she should be president. However, the popular vote margin came from California, the ultra-liberal state that allowed illegals to vote.

California population is 65 times larger than many smaller states like Vermont, Wyoming, and the Dakotas. This majority could win most elections if the popular vote were used. The Founding Fathers recognized this problem, and selected the Electoral College as the solution.

At the time the Constitution was written in 1797, the state of Virginia had ten times more people than Georgia, and Virginia could determine the election just as California could today. With the strange government in California, one wonders if the nation really wants California to determine the presidential elections.

Hillary won 48% of the popular vote to Trump's 46%, but when Hillary makes this point she forgets that Trumps' 46% was higher than Bill Clinton's popular vote of 43% in the 1992 election. Donald Trump's margin over her husband was greater than Hillary's. Another caveat on the popular vote: Abraham Lincoln only won 39% of the popular vote in 1860, but he turned out to be one of the greatest presidents in the nation's history. Trump's first year in office has produced a much stronger economy, record consumer confidence, GDP growth of 4%, illegal immigrants declining by 75%, record unemployment, and a strong foreign policy. Donald Trump could very well be a fine president despite the media jihad opinion to the contrary.

Donald Trump is a street fighter who learned the ropes with negotiations in the tough New York construction business. This experience helped in the anti-Trump environment during the election. It is doubtful that any other candidate could have survived the media attacks and the illegal Clinton and FBI tactics. He was strong, aggressive, and unrelenting in the campaign, and disposed of sixteen capable Republicans in the primaries, and Hillary Clinton in the election.

Donald Trump's accomplishments during the primaries and the election were remarkable. He won the fighting a battle with Hillary Clinton who was accepted by most to be the sure winner. The forecasters ignored Hillary's baggage; she was actually not electable.

While Hillary was only competing with Bernie Sanders, the Republican field included senators, governors, a brain surgeon, and a female CEO. The Republican field was stronger than the Democrat candidates. Hillary took over the DNC to beat Bernie, but Trump won honestly.

In addition to winning over the other candidates, it was necessary for Trump to beat the media jihad. No other candidate in history had ever defeated the media, although Harry Truman came close. Donald Trump made *fake news* his byword, and survived the worst negative media attempts in history. For some reason, the media hated Trump. They ignored the other Republican candidates, but attacked Trump with a passion. The media venom against Trump was the worst in the history of American politics.

The media was not the only group against Donald Trump. Most Washington politicians were against Trump because of his plan to *drain the swamp* in Washington. Congress did not want an *outsider* to change their lifestyle; politicians were against draining the swamp.

With this group against him, Trump certainly needed some Washington friends, but they were hard to find. However, Donald Trump had been successful in the tough New York construction business, and he was up to the task.

He was determined to listen to voters, and fix the anemic economy. His theme was to *Make America Great Again.* Hillary discounted his

Idea during the campaign, claiming *those days are gone.* In addition to her other problems, this claim did not sit well with voters.

The Democrats, the government, and the media jihad pulled out all stops in their attempts to kill Donald Trump's election, but they failed to get Hillary elected. Trump paid attention to the voters during his nationwide rallies, while Hillary was stuck in the mud with her lack of a realistic campaign strategy, and continuing with the Obama policies.

The Trump victory was even a surprise for many in the Republican National Committee; some were packing up their personal belongings when the voting started. The RNC was even sending out email messages saying *it's not our fault.* When the voting began showing a favorable trend, the chicken-hearted supporters changed into fair-weather friends.

The Trump victory was his own doing. He changed campaign managers four times, and there were always changes going on with other staff managers.

When the Associated Press announced the Trump victory at 2:33 am on Wednesday November 9, the election battle was over. The media jihad had done all they could to elect Hillary, but their efforts had failed. The personal attacks, character assassinations, assaults on his family, and non-stop criticisms had been unsuccessful. Never in the history of American politics had the media been so nasty and disgusting.

The Democrats used every trick available to eliminate both Democrat and Republican threats to Hillary's election. Bernie Sanders, the main Democrat threat, was forced to drop out because Hillary cut his campaign funds. Hillary had taken over the DNC and cut off campaign funds for Sanders. Hillary disposed of the Bernie Sanders threat, and Donald Trump was supposed to fall by the wayside with the Hillary funded Russia dossier, but the fake news dossier attempt failed. The illegal FBI Spygate by James Comey also failed. Hillary was using all her assets in the government to damage Trump, but he was still in the race.

Hillary's next threat was Donald Trump, and she planned to eliminate him with her fabricated dossier. Using the DNC as a front, Hillary used $12.4 million of the DNC money to pay an unscrupulous firm to write a document accusing

Trump of collusion with Russia. Even though the 32-page dossier was false, her friends in the FBI used the *dossier* to spy on the Trump campaign office. Despite the widespread claim of Trump collusion with Russia and the FBI Spygate, Hillary failed to eliminate Donald Trump.

The Federal Government interference in the 2016 election included the FBI and the CIA, the supposed *intelligence agencies.* Both lost credibility in the 9-11 World Trade Center attack. The FBI allowed visas for the terrorists, and failed to check their months of aircraft flight training. THE CIA failed to investigate the terrorists in Saudi Arabia, and allowed them to enter the country without documentation.

Many Americans lost respect for the FBI and CIA because of the lack of accomplishment. When the public finally found out that both agencies attempted to rig the 2016 elections, the silent majority was after blood.

The FBI attempted to damage Trump and help Hillary by spying on the Trump campaign office. This was, of course, illegal. FBI Director James Comey was personally in charge of the Clinton email investigation, but allowed Hillary to avoid jail. The DOJ was also involved with the Fusion dossier.

The Hillary email investigation by the FBI was a sham. Despite finding her guilty of transferring classified data on her personal server, Comey refused to prosecute. The FBI found 112 emails that were deleted by Hillary that had classified data, and Comey stated that Hillary was *extremely careless* in handling classified documents. His original position was that Hillary was *grossly negligent* with classified data – quite a different statement.

The Comey conclusions in Hillary's email scandal were a joke. First, Hillary deleted 30,000 emails *after* Congress subpoenaed her emails, and then lied to the FBI. However, FBI Director Comey made the decision not to indict Hillary for her crimes since it would take her out of the presidential election.

The entire FBI *investigation* was rigged right from the beginning; the rewritten FBI report that changed the classified data crime from *gross negligence* to *extremely careless* proved this point. If a normal, or regular, FBI investigation had found that an average American had mishandled classified material, the individual would have been prosecuted and put in jail. Not only did Hillary mishandle classified data, she also lied to the FBI, which is another felony. Comey intentionally changed the charges to allow Hillary to go scot-free.

The FBI fraud did not end there; Comey also spied on Donald Trump's campaign office. The false dossier was used to obtain warrants from the FISA court to spy on Trump. This illegal act was worse than Watergate.

Despite no evidence of any Trump connection with Russia, Comey used the false dossier to start an investigation of Trump's involvement with Russia. The FBI actions were attempts to fix the 2016 election. The election fix was hidden during the election, so voters were unaware of the of the criminal FBI activities. Comey, and Deputy Director McCabe were fired because of their involvement in the fix.

The CIA was also involved in the anti-Trump government programs. The agency that started the Iraq war with the (lack of) *intelligence* report that Saddam Hussein had weapons of mass destruction, was also involved in attempts to damage Trump. CIA Director John Brennan continually criticized Trump and praised Hillary, and was forced to resign after lying to Congress.

Bruce Ohr of the DOJ was instrumental in hiring Fusion GPS to produce the false Russia dossier. Ohr's wife Nellie worked for Fusion. Hillary and the DNC paid Fusion $12.4 million to develop the Trump-Russia connection in the dossier.

Emails discovered after the election proved that the 2016 election was fraudulent and corrupt. The individuals involved with the corruption, Hillary, Comey, McCabe, and Brennan, were able to hide their actions for a year, but their illegal activities eventually surfaced. Donald Trump was right when he said the election was *rigged.*

The corruption in the 2016 election was not unveiled until after the election, and if Hillary had been elected, the wrongdoing would not have surfaced; the fraud would not have been uncovered. Whistleblowers finally told the unsavory story after the election, and the distasteful plot is still under investigation.

There has always been a double standard for the Clintons going back to their days in Arkansas. The scandals accumulated over the years, but were discounted by the media.

Bill and Hillary have dodged accountability for forty years. Bill Clinton was impeached, but the reprimand was ignored. Hillary's malicious misconduct in the Benghazi tragedy was also neglected. The 2016 election involved the dossier claims about Donald Trump, but ignored the Russia connection with the Clintons.

Despite the corrupt tactics, Donald Trump, the candidate *who could never win,* was elected the 45th President of the United States.

CHAPTER FIVE
POST ELECTION

Democrats vs President Trump

The election of Donald Trump completely
changed Washington politics. Instead of
business as usual, with Wall Street and lobbyists
in control, Trump was in charge. However, since
election night, November 8, 2016, Democrats
and the media jihad developed a plan to
sabotage the President.

Democrat leaders in Congress, Chuck Schumer,
and Nancy Pelosi started building their own wall.
This was a well-constructed, political wall, with
Democrats and non-Trump Republicans on one
side, and the President on the other side.

Wall against President Trump

A political war started with Schumer and Pelosi acting as the generals; the courts and the media jihad were the lackeys. The Berlin Wall began August 31, 1961 to keep East Germans from defecting to the West, and lasted until 1989. The Democrat Wall started November 9, 2016, and will certainly last until the 2020 election.

The generals did not wait until Trump took office; they began their anti-Trump strategy immediately after election night. The media jihad against Trump did not die away with the election, it only got stronger. The *discredit the President* team went to work immediately, and their underhanded plan was to impeach President Trump. An angry and forceful team of terrorists could not be any stronger in their effort to kill President Trump's chances of success.

Just as the East German guards killed innocent people attempting to reach their neighbors in the West, Schumer and Pelosi were determined to kill all Trump legislation. The Democrat war was serious, and brought Washington to a standstill. The Federal Government offices were essentially closed; absolutely nothing was getting done.

The Schumer dirty tricks started the day after Donald Trump was elected on November 9, 2016, and continue today. The Schumer-Pelosi strategy was to stand in the way of everything the President attempted. When he submitted individuals for Cabinet positions to the Senate, Schumer, the Senate minority leader, used the filibuster to delay approval as long as possible. The Schumer block was used on every Trump appointee, and delayed approval to the point that the President was forced to work without his Cabinet members and other key officials. Schumer was ruthless in his anti-Trump program.

The Schumer-Pelosi *Resistance Wall* worked to perfection, and has continued to work throughout post-election period. Their objective is to block anything and everything President Trump attempts, even legislation that benefits all Americans.

The duo attempted to stop tax reform that provided tax reductions for most Americans. President Trump succeeded in getting the tax bill approved after a full-court press, but Schumer and Pelosi complained ad nauseam, with the argument that tax cuts only help the *rich.* A fact check proved both wrong; the tax rate or individuals earning over $400,000 remained the same as before the tax change – 35%.

Trump's *Tax Cuts and Jobs Act (TGJA)* was submitted to Congress on November 2, 2017, and was finally approved on December 22, 2017, just in time for Christmas. In addition to taxpayers receiving a reduction in taxes, jobs will increase by 0.6% or the years 2018 through 2027, and GDP will triple Obama's 1.7%.

After the tax cut legislation was passed, firms brought profits that had been held oversees because of the high tax rates, back to the U.S. Apple brought $250 billion back to the nation, and will invest over $350 billion in a new campus facility that will add 20,000 new jobs. Other firms increased their capital expenditure plans that will add new facilities and new jobs, and small businesses will receive $1.1 billion in net benefits.

In addition to individual tax cuts, new jobs, and the GDP increase, consumer spending immediately increased, and the economy took off. Democrats complaining that only the rich would benefit from the tax cuts were dead wrong. American workers immediately received bonuses from their companies, and their take-home pay increased for the first time in decades.

The American public loved the Trump tax cut legislation. High taxes had been the Democrat policy since the days of Alexander Hamilton, but the high-tax policy had stifled the economy for decades. President Trump, the non-politician, who was not capable of being president, saved the nation from the weak Obama economic policies.

Trump Tax Cuts

The Democrats, with Chuck Schumer and Nancy Pelosi at the helm, refused to accept that the Trump tax cuts were a godsend for the economy. The two political clowns, along their 243 wacko Democrats in Congress, refused to acknowledge the amazing improvements in the economy. The economy actually started taking off the day after the election. The economy was in the pits during Obama's eight-year reign, and this was one of the reasons Donald Trump won. The hard heads in the Democratic Party refuse to accept reality.

President Trump's foreign policy actions have also been phenomenal. President Obama and his lieutenants Hillary Clinton and John Kerry made the worst foreign policy mistakes in the nation's history. The Iran and North Korea nuclear threats were ignored, and both enemy nations gained ground developing a nuclear arsenal. President Obama's rhetoric was ridiculous.

President Trump took a hard line stand against both countries. North Korea was launching missiles every two weeks, with many shooting over Japan and South Korea, the U.S. allies. North Korea's Kim Jong Un even threated the U.S. in a televised speech on New Year's Day

2018. Kim reported that North Korea had completed its nuclear capability, and *the nuclear button is always on my desk in my office.* President Trump immediately replied *I also have a nuclear button, and mine is bigger and it works.* President Trump announced that the U.S. could bomb North Korea into oblivion.

North Korea's Kim Jong Un's Nuclear Button

President Trump cut of all shipments to North Korea, and urged China and other countries to do the same. The result was a dramatic drop in North Korea's economy, and Kim Jong Un was unable to do anything about it.

In April 2018, Kim Jong Un announced that North Korea was suspending its missile program, and would stop work on his nuclear program. The North Korean Leader did an about face, and cancelled his nuclear threat.

President Trump's North Korea actions will end the 68-year Korean War, and eliminate the North Korean nuclear threat. The astounding feat will go down in history as one of the most important foreign relations accomplishments in world history. Pundits were suddenly recommending that Donald Trump should receive the Nobel Peace Prize.

President Trump with the Nobel Peace Medal

After bottling up Washington, and holding up legislation, the two generals and the 243 Democrat minions in Congress, went to work on keeping the contemptible Obamacare health care fiasco in place. Trump had campaigned on repealing the failed system, and the voters agreed. Only Democrats wanted to keep Obamacare; not one Republican had voted for the *Affordable Care Act* in 2009. Democrats had the majority in Congress and pushed the health care bill through without reading the 20,000 page legislation. Obamacare had always been a political problem, but it became *non-affordable.* The cost had doubled.

The Democrats were not interested in the cost problem or Americans, their interest was to block any legislation proposed by President Trump. In addition to the infamous 245 Democrats, several renegade Republicans voted against repealing Obamacare. Trump's enemy Senator McCain of Arizona was one of the renegades.

The cost of Obamacare in Arizona was the highest in the nation, but traitor McCain voted against President Trump, and left his constituents out in the cold.

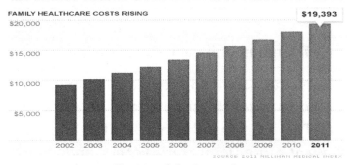

Family Health Care Costs

The notorious 245 rejected the repeal of Obamacare, and won another battle with President Trump. Costs will continue to increase, and Americans will continue to suffer.

Another campaign promise by Trump was to build a wall along the Southern border with Mexico to prevent illegal immigrants from crossing the border. Criminals and drug cartels were known to enter the U.S. in droves by simply walking across the border. Trainloads of illegals lined up at the border, and entered the country. Many were from South America and moved through Mexico to enter the United States.

Trainload of Illegals Entering the U.S.

Democrats demand that illegal immigrants be allowed to enter the country and be allowed to vote. This is against the law, but the infamous 245 want more Democratic voters, and ignore immigration laws.

A week after being sworn in as President, Donald Trump issued an executive order to limit entry of immigrants from seven Muslim countries. The next day, a Federal Court judge objected to the executive order because individuals could face *substantial and irreparable injury.* The judge obviously favored terrorists rather than American citizens.

On Sunday January 29, two days after the executive order was issued, *Shutdown Schumer* demanded that President Trump *rescind the mean-spirited and un-American order.* The video showed Schumer with tears in his eyes; he deserved an Oscar for that performance.

One week after the executive order was signed, a U.S. Federal District Judge issued a restraining order to halt implementing Trump's executive order limiting immigration.

The President has the authority to *suspend the entry of all aliens for such period of time he shall deem necessary and Presidential authority shall not be second-guessed by the courts.* The courts apparently believe they have authority over the executive and legislative branches, but the Constitution certainly does not give them that jurisdiction.

The Trump travel ban case went to the Supreme Court and almost a year after the President lawfully signed the executive order, the court allowed full implementation of the revised travel ban. The wasted year allowed illegal immigrants to pour across the border. The ultra-liberal courts need a change in personnel.

Russia was also the big news topic during the post-election period. Hillary's fake news dossier remained the media jihad answer to *what to do about Donald Trump.* The Trump-Russia collusion theme was the daily subject in the White House press conferences. The journalists sat in the same chairs every day, and repeated the same drivel. Similar to a puppet show, the media people appeared to be on the same string.

Hillary's Dossier

In an attempt to dig up dirt on Donald Trump during the election, Hillary and the DNC paid a dirt-gathering firm Fusion GPS to develop a Russia connection with Trump. The DOJ recommended Fusion; a top official's wife worked for Fusion. Christopher Steele, a former British spy who had worked in Russia was hired by Fusion to do the dirty work.

Steele produced a 17 memos claiming Trump had been involved with Russian agents conspiring to damage Hillary. The first of the documents, named the dossier, was released in June 2016, just in time for the election.

When the dossier was checked for accuracy, it was proven a fabrication. The individuals supposedly in meetings with Trump denied the accusation, and proved they were in another location when the supposed meetings were held. Steele's sources were not identified, and experts proclaimed the entire dossier a fabrication.

Even the Trump-hating media refused to report the dossier, and Hillary was concerned that the $12 million was down the drain. She needed ammunition to shoot down the threat to her long awaited presidency.

Enter John McCain, another Trump hater. McCain sent an aide to London to get a copy of the dossier, and passed copies to Comey, another Trump hater, and to members of Congress. Since McCain says he is a Republican, the media immediately accepted the dossier as gospel, and made Trump-Russia the hot topic.

The fictitious dossier was suddenly acceptable news – as the warden in the 1994 movie *The Shawshank Redemption* would say, *it's a miracle.*

Republican John McCain

The media jihad picked up the Trump-Russia dossier and ran with it; the supposed Trump connection became the main topic in the election, and throughout the post-election period.

Democrats even used the Trump Russia CDfoolishness as an impeachment tool against President Trump. The 245 Democrats in Congress had decided that impeachment of President Trump was exactly the plan to deride the President until the 2020 presidential election. Democrat members of Congress actually made long speeches claiming that Trump was not qualified to be president because of the Russia matter, and called for impeachment.

The media jihad made the Trump-Russia issue the daily news feature, and the Russia topic continued throughout 2018 - it never went away. It is truly astounding that a political ploy developed by a distrustful firm, and paid for by the DNC and Hillary, could become the main subject of a presidential election.

CLINTON, DNC PAID FOR DIRT; RUSSIAN DOSSIER
DRUDGE REPORT

Democrats and the media jihad will keep the fake news Russia issue in the news until the 2020 presidential election in an attempt to win. However, with President Trump's amazing accomplishments, the Democrats are swimming upstream. Trump has fixed the economy, and this was the main issue in the 2016 election. The President's foreign policy accomplishments have eliminated the *not presidential* argument, so the Democrats are unable to find another beef.

The American public has tired of the continuous Russia topic, and has tuned the media and the Democrats out. The 2018 mid-term election will give an indication as to how angry the silent majority is with the Russia farce.

The post-election vaudeville started immediately after the election. Democrats woke up Wednesday morning, November 9, 2016 with the biggest headache ever. Donald Trump had defeated Hillary Clinton. The Trump victory was unacceptable to those who expected their sure-fire candidate to win. They had been predicting a Hillary win for four years, but the forecasts turned sour.

Democrats were so pro-Hillary that they were oblivious to reality – Hillary was, and is today, not electable.

Hillary may think she has a chance to run for president again, thinking the third time is a charm, but it will never happen. Hillary Clinton simply has too much baggage. The loss to Trump was her second time around; she also lost to Obama in 2008, a fact ignored by the DNC, and most Democrats. The die-hard Hillary followers were so enamored with her that they failed to notice her weaknesses. Democrats completely ignored her baggage, and this was a fatal error.

The post-election period was also unkind to FBI Director Comey. He was fired by President Trump in May 2017, and even though he attempted to explain his actions during the election, few were paying attention. His email fiasco, and spying on Trump's campaign office left him nowhere to run.

Comey was working against Trump during the election even though the protocol was for the FBI to be unbiased. He overstepped his authority in the email investigation in his attempt to protect Hillary from prosecution on the handling of classified material. Kristian Saucier, the submarine sailor, was sentenced to jail for taking pictures of classified material. Hillary got off scot-free.

FBI Director James Comey

Comey was guilty of preventing prosecution for Hillary's classified material crime, and his ruling received severe criticism. His personal judgement usurped the authority of the Attorney General. Law scholars criticized Comey's actions, and Congress began an investigation in 2018.

The Watergate break-in of 1972 is considered the worst political scandal in the nation's history. However, Comey topped Watergate with spying on the Trump campaign office; the only thing missing were the *plumbers.*

James Comey also used Hillary's false dossier that included the Clinton lies about Trump to obtain warrants from a FISA court. The warrants allowed the FBI to spy on Trump during the election. Trump complained that his *wires were tapped,* but the crime was ignored. The FBI hid *Spygate,* but it was exposed in 2017.

The FBI *secret mission* to spy on the Trump headquarters failed to work, but Spygate never became an issue during the election. The FBI hid their tracks. The use of the FISA court was illegal. FISA is limited to *foreign intelligence,* and has no authority for spying on U.S. citizens; the warrant was also illegal.

The FBI deliberately broke the law by lying to the FISA judge and using the false dossier to justify the warrants. Congress started an investigation of the entire FISA activity in 2017, but with Democrats protecting Comey it appears that nothing will be done.

The *Washington Post* created the Watergate scandal by digging into the Republican attempt to break into the DNC office. Unlike Watergate, the media jihad refused to pursue the spying on the Trump campaign office. Evidently, there will not be another *All the President's Men* movie.

As the facts of the election are exposed, there are never ending investigations. However, a Special Counsel should certainly investigate the Coney spy tactic. It is truly amazing that the FBI Director would be involved in politics, and go to such lengths to destroy Trump; he obviously knew the spying was illegal.

When Comey used the fake news dossier to obtain warrants to spy on Trump without checking the validity of the document, he was really going to the limit. He also knew that spying on Trump was illegal, and he was taking a big chance with his reputation. The dossier was a fairy tale created by Hillary to damage her opponent, and he knew it.

Comey also used the Steele and Hillary lies about President Trump to start a Special Counsel investigation of President Trump. For the first time in history, a Special Council was appointed to investigate the President of the United States with absolutely no evidence of him doing anything wrong; the dossier was a joke.

The two-year FBI investigation found no evidence of any connection between Trump and Russia, and Mueller's yearlong inquiry also failed to find any Trump collusion. The amazing thing is that the investigations continue.

As expected, Hillary blamed the email scandal on the *right wing conspiracy,* and dodged any responsibility for using her private server when she was secretary of state. She used the server to keep her emails secret, and burned over 30,000 emails *after* a subpoena by Congress.

Lying to the FBI is a felony, and most people would be in jail, but not Hillary; the FBI made sure she stayed in the presidential race.

The media jihad continued the fake news dossier claim after the election. The White House press conferences became yesterday's news when reporters constantly pursued the Trump-Russia questions. Mueller indicted thirteen Russian agents for their interference in the 2016 election, but Putin said the individuals were not even Russians.

The timing of the Special Counsel indictments was interesting. With the mainstream media continuous inquiries about a Trump-Russia connection, the subject was daily fake news, and Mueller was on the hot seat to indict somebody. The three years of FBI and Mueller investigations found absolutely nothing on Donald Trump, so Mueller chose to indict the supposed Russians.

The Russia indictments were meaningless; the Russians certainly would not choose to come to America and subject themselves to a U.S. trial. The Mueller indictment announcement was strictly a political ploy to feed the media frenzy. The post-election fake news remained the same; it was as if the election never happened.

The Russia involvement in the 2016 election is not new. Russia, China, and many countries interfere in elections, including America. Obama used $350,000 of taxpayer money in an attempt to defeat Netanyahu in 2015, a well-known fact. The U.S. also interfered in Chile's elections in the 1960s, and instigated the overthrow of South Korea's government in the 1970s. The U.S. involvement in other nation's elections has been going on for decades, but has never received media attention until Hillary used the Russia-Trump connection in her campaign.

The 2018 Special Counsel indictments will certainly cause the media to continue their crusade against President Trump. Democrats in Congress immediately began their rhetoric about President Trump, but conveniently avoided any reference to Hillary's involvement with Russia. Hillary was directly involved with Russia when she approved the Uranium One acquisition of a U.S. uranium mining company in 2010.

The secret approval of a Russian nuclear agency obtaining 20% of a U.S. uranium firm was never exposed, and the mainstream media have conveniently ignored the Clinton-Russia involvement. It is truly amazing that the media and Democrats refuse to admit that Hillary was involved with Russia when she was secretary of state. Allowing Russia to obtain U.S. uranium was hidden by the Obama administration, and only surfaced when the book *Clinton Cash* was published in 2016.

The book goes into detail outlining the Russia payoff to Hillary for voting for the Russia acquisition of the Canadian firm Uranium One. Bill Clinton received $500,000 for a short speech in Russia while Hillary was secretary of state in 2010. He had never been involved with Russia before that time.

The next payoff was the $145 million donation to the Clinton Foundation by the CEO of Uranium One during the approval process. Any foreign involvement in a U.S. company requires approval from CIFUS, a committee assigned to review the acquisition. Hillary, as secretary of state, was an important member of CIFUS.

Hillary was against the Uranium One deal until the payoffs occurred. However, she quickly changed her tune, and approved the acquisition. Uranium One owned 20% of a U.S. uranium mining firm, so Russia gained control of America's uranium.

The FBI investigated the Clinton-Russia deal until the State Department issued a report indicating the Uranium One acquisition *did not pose a threat to U.S. security.* Of course, Hillary was the head of the State Department. President Obama also approved the Uranium One acquisition.

Why the Obama administration would ever approve the Russia acquisition of a U.S. uranium firm was never questioned since the entire process was hidden. The entire approval process is suspicious, and Congress is currently reviewing the matter. However, congressional action is always split between the two political parties, and is never an effective method for any action.

Hillary was able to dodge responsibility for a Russia connection, and used the fake news dossier to push the Russia issue to Trump. The entire process was an amazing switcheroo by the Clintons, but it was successful.

Russia is only one of the daily attacks on President Trump. He is continually accused of everything from soup to nuts without any verification. The Democrats in Congress make speeches that he is not capable of being president, and should be impeached.

Impeachment is not in the cards because it requires treason, bribery, or high crimes and misdemeanors, and President Trump is not guilty of any of these crimes. The impeachment idea is simply another Democrat UFO to keep the anti-Trump sentiment going until the 2020 elections.

The atmosphere in Washington after Trump's election was similar to a third-world coup. Democrats were doing everything they could to discredit President Trump. Their favorite candidate had lost, and bureaucrats were determined to undermine the new Republican President. The attacks were underhanded and despicable, and the media jihad added to the anti-Trump attack with their fake news. The daily malicious defamation of the President is never ending.

With the Washington bureaucrats leaking fake news to the media, the constant media jihad against the president, and the illegal FBI actions during and after the election, the Washington scene is one of massive division. President Trump attempted to make peace, but the Democrats refused to accept that he was the President of the United States. Why anyone would want to run for president is certainly a valid question.

The political games continued throughout 2017 and 2018. The President was the enemy, and everything possible was being done to stop his programs. Pelosi and Schumer were working together to block congressional legislation, and the government was in a quagmire. Schumer used filibuster tactics to prevent votes in the Senate, and Pelosi was making long anti-Trump speeches in the House. The situation was an utter disaster.

In addition to the Democrats preventing legislation, the FBI was still moving against President Trump, and the media jihad was getting worse. There was hardly any real news reported by the drive-by media; TV channels and newspapers reported the same fake news. *One America News,* and *Fox News* were the only outlets reporting the news; the other news outlets concentrated on the Trump-Russia connection ad nauseam.

The illegal FBI actions against Donald Trump were hidden during the election, but their attempts to damage his candidacy became public knowledge in 2017. Emails between two high level DOJ agents were made public proving that the FBI used illegal tactics during the election.

The mainstream media failed to report the FBI issue, but conservative news covered the debacle in detail. The emails proved that many in the FBI, including Comey and Deputy Director McCabe, conspired to elect Hillary, and discredit Donald Trump. Both Comey and McCabe were fired because of their actions, and several agents were moved into other jobs.

Some emails tied President Obama to the FBI anti-Trump actions during the election when he had asked for a full report on the FBI activity. The former President denied the report, but it is hard to believe that he was not directing the plan since the intelligence agencies were involved.

FBI Director Wray replaced Comey, and he began a reorganization of the FBI. The FBI and Justice Department lost all credibility with the public, and the new director started reorganizing the agency. However, once a government agency loses credibility, it takes a long time to regain public trust.

The mainstream media continued the jihad against President Trump, but his attacks on the fake news were effective. The public had lost trust in the media, so most of their negative tactics against the President were ignored.

The angry reporters in the White House press conference were still consistently anti-Trump, and continued with the dossier questions. The public was no longer paying attention because all the questions were the same.

The nation was divided along party lines, and the division was the worst in history; even the early years of the political parties in the 1790s were not as bad. President Trump recognized the divisive atmosphere, and was attempting to heal the division in the nation. His presidential acceptance speech began with the words: *Now is the time for Americans to heal the wounds of division.*

However, the Democrats had a different agenda, and rejected his *olive branch.* Their objective was to do everything possible to discredit the President in the attempt to win the 2020 presidential election. Four years is a long time to listen to the Democrat drivel. The public had tired of their trivial nonsense, and they were overdoing the Russia burlesque.

The Democrat team of Chuck Schumer and Nancy Pelosi led their team into the Trump battle similar to the *Charge of the Light Brigade that* resulted in 50% causalities. The infamous 245 should be careful.

Charge of the Light Brigade

What happened to patriotic politicians who are interested in America instead of their political party? The Republicans were disappointed that the underdog Harry Truman won in 1948, but they actively worked with the Democrats to pass record legislation. The 2016 Democrats did just the opposite. Not only did they block legislation with their Democrat wall, they actively pursued impeachment.

The Democrats obviously have no interest in solving the nation's problems, and continue to use politics as their legislative tool to damage the nation. There are 150 legislative bills being held up by the Democrats in Congress; Washington has essentially shut down. The 115th Congress may as well go back where they came from because they are not doing anything.

How Schumer could be so divisive is difficult to understand, but he certainly allowed his political feelings to interfere with his job as Senate Minority leader. Nancy Pelosi did the same as the House Minority leader. The Democrats essentially blocked the government with their wall of opposition.

The Democrats also stopped the 2018 budget. The government fiscal year begins October 1 of each year; when the 2018 budget was sent to the Senate for approval in September 2017, Schumer refused to agree with the budget unless DACA and the Dream Act legislation was approved.

The DACA legislation allows illegal immigrants who entered the country as minors to receive amnesty, and be eligible to work. The Dreamers legislation, Development, Relief, and Education, for Alien Minors, allows illegal immigrants to gain permanent residency. Democrats were putting illegal immigrants ahead of American citizens in the attempt to increase the number of Democratic voters in the country. The Schumer-Pelosi tag team never mentions the fact that illegal immigrant entry is against the law; instead, they accuse Republicans of being un-American.

The continuous debates about immigration and the budget were nauseous. The silent majority realizes that the Democrat push for illegals is to gain more Democrat voters, and ignore the media and Democrat push for illegal entry.

Schumer finally shut the government down in 2018. The demand by Democrats that illegal immigrants be allowed to vote was refused by President Trump. He wanted immigration law to be enforced, and the silent majority agreed with the President.

The entire Democrat plan for immigration was simply politics; Schumer and Pelosi used the DACA and Dreamers fiasco to stop President Trump's plan to build a wall. Voters' elected Trump and agreed with the wall.

The Democrats were playing politics to gain more Democratic voters with illegal immigrants. Immigration law prohibits non-citizens from voting in federal elections, with penalties of imprisonment and deportation. However, some states are lenient, and give voting rights to undocumented aliens. California even passed a law (AB 60) that allows illegal immigrants to obtain a driver's license, and this gives the individuals automatic voter registration. Some states do not even require a driver's license for identification. The lack of identification for voting allows practically anyone to vote.

The Democrat members of Congress, elected to represent the people in their state to uphold the law, violate the law. What happened to integrity – the Democrats certainly have ignored that principle. Their idea that the nation should close their eyes to the law is unbelievable.

Trump suggested that a wall be built along the southern border to prevent illegal immigrants from bringing drugs into the country. Millions of illegals from Mexico and South America simply walk across the border into California, Arizona, New Mexico, and Texas, and it is impossible to stop the entry without a wall.

Illegals Crossing into the U.S.

While 75% of Americans agreed with the wall, Schumer, Pelosi, and their merry group of Democrats were determined to stop any funding for the wall. Democrats were demanding approval of DACA and Dreamers legislation as the method to allow illegal immigrants to enter the nation. Evidently, their belief that gaining additional Democrat voters is more important than protecting the American public.

The Democrats were penalizing American citizens, and favoring illegal immigrants with their attempt to bring in more illegal immigrants to vote with the Democratic Party. The ultra-liberal mainstream media never report this issue, and continue to support the Democrat plan. The media jihad against the President makes the problem even worse.

Hillary lost the election, and she took the loss hard; she could not believe the voters had rejected her claims that she would be a great president. She blamed everybody and everything, but not herself. The latest count is 36 individuals caused her to lose the election. She was expected to blame others, but 36 is ridiculous. The loss was a hard pill to swallow. Her book *What Happened* listed all *her* reasons for losing, but conveniently left out the lack of truthfulness, which was the most damaging issue in her baggage.

Hillary also lost her first chance to be president when Obama beat her in the 2008 primaries, so this was her second defeat. Her two defeats were caused by the same problem: Hillary Clinton is simply not electable.

Hillary's 469-page book was published in 2017, and was a self-defense memoir for her loss to Donald Trump. She listed her reasons for losing, but never indicated she may have been the real reason. Hillary had researched her loss to Obama in 2008 in an attempt to do better in 2016. Her ego forced her to ignore the truthfulness problem, and it got to her again in 2016.

The Russia interference in the election was on page one of her book, even though there is no evidence that Russia had any effect on the election. Russia is suspected of hacking into the DNC, but the systems were not protected – everybody hacked into DNC computers. The polls are decentralized and not connected to the internet, so it impossible to fix an election. No evidence exists that the Russians affected the 2016 election.

Bernie Sanders was included in *Hillary's List,* along with most everybody else, but Bernie dropped out of the race on July 12, 2016, two weeks before the Democratic National Convention. The timing of Bernie's drop out would indicate that he had little to do with Hillary losing the election. Interesting that the illegal takeover of the DNC by the Clintons was not mentioned in her book.

Despite FBI Director Comey spying on the Trump campaign office to help Hillary, he also made Hillary's list. Comey put his career in jeopardy with his attempts to help Hillary with the email and Spygate activities, and was later fired for his actions. It is difficult to see how Hillary could blame Comey for *her* loss, but she continues to tour the world blaming everybody but herself for losing the election.

Even though the email and Benghazi scandals were definitely her fault, Hillary blamed the issues on the mysterious *right wing conspiracy.* The 40-year old excuse was wearing thin with voters.

Hillary also blamed Julian Assange for releasing her emails, but she failed to mention that her private server was hacked because it was not secure.

193

Hillary's entire book was a fairy tale of excuses, and has received negative reports. The media and pundits have attempted to find excuses for Trump's win and Hillary's loss, but none arrived at the electability issue.

Hillary conveniently omitted any reference to lack of truthfulness in her book. The right wing conspiracy was always the reason for her many scandals. She also failed to mention that the Clintons paid for the fake news dossier and included her criticisms of Donald Trump in the document. Donald Trump's supposed Russia connection continues to be Hillary's main excuse for losing the election.

The media jihad and Democrat hard-liners continue to accuse President Trump of damaging Hillary's chances during the election with unverified Russia issues. The Mueller Special Counsel is still investigating the Russia affair despite no evidence of any Trump involvement. The fake news dossier still dominates the political scene sixteen months after the election and will continue until Trump leaves office.

The FBI interference in the 2016 election was illegal, and clearly showed the Washington bias against Donald Trump. Obama's administration used every trick in the book to assure Hillary's election. James Comey, the Director of the FBI, and John Brennan, the Director of the CIA were the main culprits. Prior elections were tainted, but never before had the government agencies been directly involved with fixing a presidential election.

Hillary and the DNC dreamed up the Russia-Trump connection as a tool to attack Trump, and the FBI and CIA used the false dossier in attempts to rig the election. These tactics are common in third-world country elections, but never before in the United States. The Trump accusation that the election was *rigged* hit the nail on the head, but the media ignored it.

Instead of taking the defeat gracefully, and attempting to reshape her baggage, Hillary continued her campaign against President Donald Trump. The hate crusade continued throughout 2017 and into 2018, but even her favorite media friends tired of the struggle and limited her appearances on television. However, she continued her efforts to discredit President Trump throughout her worldwide book tour. It appears that Hillary will go to her grave blaming her loss on everybody but herself.

The media jihad never stops; despite Hillary losing and Trump winning in November 2016, the negative articles on Donald Trump still appear daily. The anti- Trump media continues to report the Russia matter. The continuous attacks on Trump are getting old, and the public ignores the fake news. The media is losing influence with voters because much of the media rhetoric is so obviously biased and over the top. President Trump fights the fake news media at every turn, and continues to win more than he loses.

Trump's continuous fake news tweets kept the media chasing his bait. The press corps who attend the White House conferences appear comical with their anti-Trump questions.

Press secretary Sarah Huckabee is required to put up with ridiculous questions, and does a great job of putting each reporter in their proper place. The White House press conferences are turning most viewers off, and should die away.

Reporters are recognized to be ultra-liberal, but many go out of their way to be obnoxious; they look ridiculous in doing so. The reporters in the press conferences appear to be oblivious of how stupid they look. Possibly their true persona shows.

The media picked Donald Trump as their main target as soon as he announced he would be running for president in June 2015. Jeb Bush and Scott Walker indicated their intention to run earlier than Trump, and were the early favorites, but neither received the ruthless media outrage. The continuous vicious media attacks on a political candidate are unprecedented.

The reason for the hatred of Donald Trump has never been explained, but some reporter could very well win a Pulitzer if he/she uncovers the truth. However, the jihad is definitely there, and the entire media are together doing everything they can to destroy Donald Trump. They fail to recognize however, that Donald Trump is tough to bring down.

Donald Trump had been attacked by the media before, recognized the media bias early on, and immediately fought back. His continual tweets about fake news put the media on the defensive. While the term fake news may not be new, Trump made it part of our everyday dictionary. The media often misquoted Trump, and he immediately responded with his exact words, pointing out the errors in the media reports.

Trump's response to the mainstream media was new; the media had always controlled the information fed to the public without any return from the individual receiving their attacks. However, Donald Trump has the intestinal fortitude to nail the media for fake news.

The silent majority refused to watch the fake news channels and ignored the liberal *New York Times* and *Washington Post.* The public tends to agree with Trump, and the media outlets have suffered a drop in public acceptance.

Another issue with the media is that news outlets have turned to individuals classified as *experts* to give their opinions. The days of Walter Cronkite are gone. The famous CBS news anchor reported the news for twenty years, and was known as *the most trusted man in America.*

Except for Graham Ledger of One America News, there is no successor for Walter Cronkite. Ledger comes close to Cronkite with news reporting. Other news anchors pass the ball to their *contributors* to give their *opinions.* In most cases, the news outlets have a panel of three or four *contributors* to report the news. Often the contributors give their biased opinions rather than reporting the facts.

Viewers don't want opinions, they want a report on the news. For some unknown reason, the opinion idea is common with all news outlets today, but television viewers and newspaper readers tune them out.

Many Americans feel that it is impossible to get a realistic news report anymore. *One America News* gives unbiased news, and *Fox News* claims to be fair and balanced in their news reports, but *Fox* uses their so-called expert contributors to give their opinions of the news.

The media jihad against President Trump is as tiring as yesterday's news, and it never ends. The press continually criticizes the President, but ignores his changes that have accomplished near miracles in the economy and foreign policy. The improvements in the war against ISIS have also been missed; the media jihad is so focused on Trump that they ignore the worldwide news.

The media have ignored the astonishing improvements in the economy; it is as if it never happened. The Obama unemployed are working high-paying jobs, and they surely notice the improvement. All 401k investors have seen an increase in their portfolios despite the downturn in the DOW in early 2018. Small businesses have seen a big drop in government regulations, and have added workers and investment. The unemployment rate of 3.8% is the lowest in 25 years; minority unemployment is the best in history. There has been a 75% decline in illegal immigrants with Trump's support of the Border Control. It is amazing the media fails to report the improvements.

The media jihad group deliberately refuses to report the Trump accomplishments in foreign relations. They have ignored the miracle with North Korea. Kim Jong Un threatened the U.S. with nuclear attacks in January 2018, but the President came back with the threat to bomb North Korea *into oblivion.* Kim Jong Un then changed his pitch; he cancelled his weekly missile launches, and made peace with South Korea. He also said he would stop his nuclear program if the U.S. would not bomb his country.

The North Korea nuclear threat was a world problem, and President Trump destroyed their nuclear wall similar to Reagan tearing down the Berlin wall. This is one of the leading foreign policy achievements in history. Pundits recognized the accomplishment, and suggested that President Trump receive the Nobel Peace Prize.

The media needs to remove their blinders and report the news. Their bias reporting did not deter Donald Trump, and had little effect on the election. No matter how hard they worked to obliterate Donald Trump, he survived, and delivered a knockout punch to Democrats and the media favorite, Hillary Clinton.

Possibly the Hillary loss was such a blow to the media pride that they continue the anti-Trump jihad; they do have a huge ego. They should be concerned about how history will look at their jihad efforts.

George Washington certainly did not deserve Colonial newspaper fake news criticisms of his heroics in the Revolutionary War. Trump is no George Washington, but he and his family do not deserve the crude attacks. The media can be vicious.

There is a similarity between the media and the government – there is no accountability. Both continue in their underhanded ways without any oversight. The voters can eventually vote the politicians out of office, but it takes a long time. The public is also the only group that oversees the media, and their only tool for correction is to stop reading or watching the product.

This eventually drives the media to either change of go bankrupt, but this also takes a long time. There is no tool for the public to change the spark plugs in the media. Neither Congress nor the media has any accountability, and their headaches are difficult to correct.

Both the politicians and the media ignore the silent majority, and they have separated themselves from their audience. They evidently fail to see this as a problem.

Immigration will be an issue in the upcoming election. The Democrat position of allowing illegal immigrants to enter the country just to gain additional voters for the Democratic Party could be a problem for the Schumer Pelosi team.

The media agenda is so anti-Trump that people are tired of the continual bashing; the jihad goes overboard with their criticism. The actual news gets little attention. President Trump allowed the military run the war against ISIS, and they have driven the terrorists out of Iraq, but liberal reporters have ignored the news. The Obama policy of dropping leaflets advising the terrorists where the next bomb will be dropped was scrapped. The jihad has totally disrupted the flow of information to the public.

The *selected news* is almost criminal, but the news' customers are fighting back by ignoring the continuous gossip and innuendos about the President. The media is continuing their attacks on President Trump with the Russia collusion issue, but losing the battle with the silent majority; they can see the biased reporting and ignore it. The Russia-Trump matter has become yesterday's news, and most Americans simply avoid the fake news.

The media has overdone the criticism of Donald Trump. The never-ending condemnation has become tiresome, and the public pays little attention to the biased rhetoric.

It is not surprising that media management has allowed the jihad to take place; the entire media industry is ultra-liberal. The media reporters are expected to be liberal because the journalism schools are ultra-liberal.

The public is not interested in the *opinions* of these people, they simply want the news. The TV stations bring on puppets to present the news the want it to be seen. The newspaper *opinion* page is always ultra-liberal, but papers also use puppets to express their opinions. Paul Krugman's opinion of Trump is an example.

Donald Trump made *draining the swamp* in Washington one of campaign promises and the voting public agreed. This idea hit a nerve with politicians because they would lose their power, and most are against changing Washington. Congress has no term limits, so elected officials are allowed to remain in office as long as they can be reelected. Some remain in office until they pass away.

Trump's drain the swamp plan offended both Democrats and Republicans because all members in Congress like the system the way it is. They can stay in power and live the comfortable life in Washington. Term limits require an amendment to the Constitution, but Congress will never pass that amendment.

Article Five of the Constitution allows the states to amend the Constitution if 75% of the states propose a change. The public have petitioned state legislators to pass congressional term limit legislation. So far, twelve states have approved legislation for term limits, and thirty other states have the issue under consideration.

There is a *revolution* in the nation against the politicians in Washington. People are tired of the do-nothing politicians who are unable to balance the budget, and can't control spending. Congress spends more than the budget every year. The politicians ignore the voters, and remain in office forever. The *Convention of States* movement plans to amend the Constitution by having 34 states (the 75% majority required) vote for congressional term limits and a balanced budget. The fat cat Washington politicians are fighting the movement, and Hillary claims the movement violates the Constitution.

Trump's drain the swamp plan will continue despite the political opposition. It will take a non-politician like President Trump to make it happen, and if the voting public continues to support him, the long-time politicians will be looking for a job.

Donald Trump refused to accept campaign contributions from people interested in a payback; in fact, he used $66 million of his own money during his campaign. Donors expect to to be repaid, and this has been a problem in Washington for decades. The demands of campaign donors have resulted in unnecessary spending legislation that drives the annual budget deficit out of control. Wall Street donated $2 billion to Hillary's campaign.

Politicians never discuss the budget and national debt during an election, probably because of the embarrassment. Congress has balanced the budget only five times in the past 60 years, and this is the main reason that the national debt is $20 trillion. The crazy thing is that the budget increases 10% every year, and Congress still spends $500 billion more than the budget every year.

Congress simply is unable to control spending. If individuals or companies increased their budget every year, and then spent more than the budget, they would be bankrupt in short order.

Congress uses a *baseline budget* system, which allows the prior year budget to be the base. Most companies' use a *zero-base budget* system in which every dollar must justified every year. The budget increases up to 10% every year for inflation and population growth, but there is no attempt to cut spending. Inflation has been less than two percent in recent years, but the budget still increases ten percent.

The national debt is another financial disaster. Obama doubled the debt during his eight years in office; the national debt is over $20 *trillion* and increases every year.

The only solution is to replace current politicians, and elect business people who can manage the economy. Term limits may be the only answer. Hopefully, the revolution movement will finally add term limits, because Congress certainly will not vote for draining the swamp. The term-limit solution appears to be the only fix because the same politicians keep getting reelected.

The media jihad against Donald Trump increased after the election, and the Democrats joined the jihad. They bonded together to stand in the way of Trump legislation, and Democrats filibustered every Trump nominee for office, even though many were Democrats.

The President was pushing through his campaign promises without any help from Congress. President Trump forced the tax cut legislation approval despite months of objections by the Democrats, and the economy soared. Businesses received a one-time tax cut from 35% to 15% for the repatriation of profits from overseas operations. This allowed the firms to bring profits back to the U.S. at a lower tax rate; the result was a tax revenue bonanza for the government. Firms increased investment in their business; Apple brought $250 billion back to the country, and then invested $350 billion in a new campus requiring 20,000 new jobs.

Democrats had objected to the lower tax rate for business for years even though the U.S tax rate for businesses was the highest in the world. The Democratic motto is tax the rich, and Democrats evidently consider business the *rich.* What a ridiculous concept; but Democrat politicians use that party line whenever taxes are discussed. The business tax cuts also allowed businesses to increase wages for workers, and many companies immediately paid bonuses to employees.

Workers will use the added income for increased spending, and this will also boost the economy. The Democrat's theory that tax reduction hurts the economy is dead wrong, yet they continue with the propaganda.

Schumer and Pelosi encouraged Democrats in Congress to reject Trump's tax reduction legislation, but Trump prevailed. Despite the improvements in the economy, lower unemployment, and worker wage increases, the Democrats still proclaim the tax-cut was a disaster for the working class.

The cost of Obamacare has doubled, and Donald Trump introduced legislation to replace the failed health care program. Democrats blocked the legislation despite the cost. The voters agreed with Trump's proposal, but the Democrat wall succeeded in canceling the bill.

The cost of Obamacare has increased to the level that people can't afford health care, and patients certainly are not able to keep their doctors. Senator McCain voted against canceling Obamacare despite the cost being double the prior year in Arizona.

Republicans in Congress objected to Obamacare for seven years, but when they finally had a president who would approve legislation to cancel Obamacare, the Republican majority failed to pass new health care legislation.

When the *Affordable Care Act* legislation was approved in March 2010, not one Republican voted for Obamacare. As it turned out, Obamacare was *not affordable.* The entire health care issue is political, with Democrats demanding that illegal immigrants be allowed health care, and Republicans unable to draft a realistic health care proposal.

Washington is broken, and needs fixing, and President Trump is the perfect individual to make this happen, but he will have to do it alone. Democrats in Congress refuse to help, and Republicans are not much better. The only hope is that the states will force term limits on Congress to get the fat cats out of Washington.

Congress has been at a standstill since the election, and the Democrats have caused the gridlock to continue. For the first time in decades, the country has a president willing and able to turn things around, but the Democrat wall is in the way. The inmates are running the prison, and are firmly against any changes.

The post-election period involved the worst conflict between the two political parties in history. Democrats used every political trick to stifle the President, and the media jihad continued their effort to damage the President on a daily basis. Politics had been bad before, but never had the opposition party been so destructive. The Will Rogers quote on political parties hit the mark: *I'm not a member of any organized political party, I'm a Democrat.*

CHAPTER SIX

DONALD TRUMP

President Donald Trump

General George S. Patton is given credit for the line: *Lead, Follow, or Get Out of the Way,* and Donald Trump followed this vernacular throughout his career. Trump also worked the axiom during his presidential campaign. His quote: *I don't need to read the polls to make decisions,* is characteristic of his approach during the election.

Trump ignored the media, the polls, the Republican Party, and just about everybody, to become the President of the United States on November 9, 2016. His victory has been reported to be a massive upset, but it only reflected the opinion of voters across the nation. The *silent majority* had tired of the do-nothing Washington politicians, and wanted a change.

It is amazing that Hillary and her campaign staff missed that voters were fed up with Washington. The mid-term elections in 2010 and 2014 certainly gave the message that voters had tired of the Obama promises of jobs when over nine million workers were out of work, and half that number had given up looking for a job. His propaganda that the economy was sound also was dead wrong with GDP growth at less than two percent. The silent majority was tired of Washington promises with no action. Hillary and the DNC missed the signals, and continued with Obama's economic policies - a big mistake.

During the campaign, Trump was vocal in his criticism of the Obama policies, and Obama backpedaling on his *line in the sand* with *Syria* was high on his list. His attacks on the Obama administration included lack of action on the economy, lack of leadership, losing rather than winning in trade, declining military strength, anemic GDP growth, and the lack of a strong foreign policy. These issues hit home with the voters, but Hillary's forum was to continue with President Obama's policies. Trump was able to identify the voters' complaints, and include corrective action plans in his platform. Hillary really did not have a plan to change anything.

Before election night, Americans suffered through two years of speeches, primaries, primary and presidential debates, one vice-presidential debate, numerous TV interviews, and constant media coverage. As election night neared, it seemed as though all media outlets in the nation covered the candidates and their families 24/7. The ritual was demanding for the candidates, but also tiresome for the voters; the pre-election bustle just took too long.

During this trying period, Donald Trump continually said he was no politician, and this was definitely true. He mistrusted the media and the pollsters, and for good reason – they were wrong; over 80% of the polls predicted a Hilary win on election night. The polling errors were a disaster, and have yet to be explained.

Washington politicians are always attempting to be politically correct whenever they are being interviewed, and in many cases, it comes out like a fairy tale. The 13% approval rating of Congress indicates that the public believes politicians to be liars. Trump is no politician, and continually said he was not interested in being politically correct, and this hit home with voters.

Politicians often begin their speeches by telling the world how poor they were in their youth. Hillary pushes the point further claiming she was *broke* when she left the White House. Her income was over $12 million that year, so Hillary surely stretches the truth.

Trump takes the opposite approach; he is proud of his accomplishments, and encourages voters to pursue the American dream. The approach worked because the public was tired of the outmoded political rhetoric.

Trump did not deny his wealth, but instead used it as the model for success. He was born into a wealthy family in 1946, and increased the family net worth with hard work. His father Fred made his money in New York real estate, and Donald followed his example. His father demanded that his children work and learn that work is required to be successful. He graduated from the Wharton School of Business in 1968 and joined his father in his real estate business.

Manhattan real estate is a tough business with daily conflicts with unions, politicians, and the impossible New York regulations. Trump learned the ropes and became highly successful. His ability to work with, and through, the conflicts of the New York business environment developed his business experience background. Donald Trump's business expertise enabled him to develop the trade and business growth policies of his 2016 election campaign.

Trump was the only one of the twenty-two presidential candidates to attack U.S. trade imbalance. The problem has existed for over sixty years, but politicians, including presidents, have done absolutely nothing. The Japanese started the problem in the 1950s with automobiles, cameras, and electronic sales. The exchange rate of 300 yen to one dollar allowed cars and components to be sold in the U.S. cheaper than in Japan – an unrealistic situation when freight and duty are included. The import problem cost U.S. manufacturing jobs; within a few years, the U.S. camera business disappeared, and foreign imports had taken fifty percent of the U.S. car and machine tool markets. Today foreign cars and trucks have over fifty percent of the U.S. vehicle market, and the loss of jobs is in the hundreds of thousands. While Japan quality is always mentioned as the reason U.S. firms lost market share, the exchange rate issue was the main problem.

Trump criticized NAFTA as being unfair to the U.S. and created trade deficits. Hillary and the other Republican candidates claimed NAFTA to be the best thing since sliced bread, but the trade deficits forced American firms to close their doors, and Trump emphasized this point. The number of U.S. workers employed in the manufacturing sector had dropped 33% since NAFTA was passed in 1994.

Most Washington politicians are attorneys, and have no idea how important manufacturing jobs are to the nation. In the 2008 congressional hearings on the auto issue, legislators actually praised the foreign carmakers, and ridiculed the Big Three. Congress had no respect for U.S. auto companies, and criticized the CEO's as if they were drug runners. Evidently, the law curriculum does not include *Business 101.*

During his rallies across the nation, Trump was highly critical of present-day politicians saying that they gave the government a bad name because nothing is ever accomplished. Trump's *America First* theme hit home with the public, and they voted him into the White House.

The Pew Research Center, a private think tank, reported that in 2016 most Americans believed that the economy had not recovered from the 2008 recession despite President Obama's continuous propaganda that he had accomplished a miracle by eliminating the financial crisis. Pew also reported that two-thirds of Americans believed that job opportunities had not increased despite Obama's four State of the Union speeches about jobs. Evidently, President Obama had his rose-colored glasses on while discussing the economy.

Hillary and the DNC drank the Obama Kool-Aid and ignored the poor economy. With nine million unemployed, and a decrease of five percent in the nation's workforce, the idea that the economy was improving was a delusion. Half the nine million had given up on finding a job. Many homeowners were still under water with their mortgages despite the $14 trillion bailout of mortgage companies, Wall Street, and 800 banks. The Treasury had panicked when the housing recession hit in 2008, and the government poured a record amount of taxpayer money into the financial community.

The unemployment rate was reported to be 5%, but few believed the number. How can the economy be great when there are nine million unemployed, and forty-eight million on food stamps.

The Congressional Budget Office increases the budget nearly 10% every year which assures that within ten years the budget will be 100% higher than today. This ridiculous budgeting process has been going on since 1974 and has increased the national debt from $475 billion to $20 trillion today.

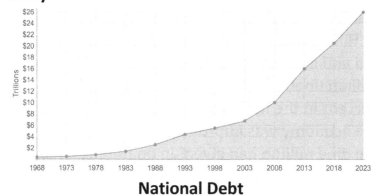

National Debt

Politicians spend an average of $500 billion more than the budget *every* year, and the budget increases up to 10% every year – ridiculous. Evidently, the country needs business people managing the budget rather than lawyers. Politicians do not have the discipline to reduce spending to balance the budget, and have been proven to be incapable of managing the finances of the government.

Trump's fiscal policies brought out another major difference between the presidential candidates. Trump continually criticized the Obama economic policies, while Hilary always praised the economy. President Obama did inherit a recession, but his efforts to fix the recession and create jobs were an utter disaster.

The GDP growth rate, the most accurate measure of economic growth, was negative much of the time, and always less than two percent during the eight-year Obama reign. The GDP growth rate during prior post-recession periods averaged over 5%. The economy never recovered from the 2008 recession, and there were more workers unemployed, and underemployed than ever. The 1992 axiom *It's the economy, stupid* certainly applied to the 2016 election situation.

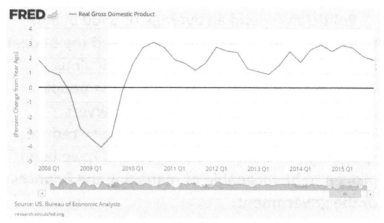

GDP Growth Rate Disaster

The GDP growth rate during Obama's eight-year reign averaged 1.7%, which is recession-era growth. The average GDP growth in the prior twenty-year period was over 3.1%; President Obama was the *only* president in the nation's history to never reach a 3% annual GDP growth rate. The difference between 1.7% and 3.1% may appear to be small, but it means a huge difference in the number of jobs, and business investments to create jobs.

The nation remained in a recession during President Obama's eight years despite his claims to the contrary. Politicians slept through the recession and post-recession period, doing absolutely nothing to help the unemployed.

Trump identified the GDP problem, promised to fix it, and he did. In his first year, the GDP growth rated reached 4% and was climbing; the DOW also had record increases. The positive turnaround in the economy was accomplished without any help from politicians in Washington, which simply proved that lawyers do not know what drives the economy, or how to manage the economy to create jobs. Congress is asleep at the wheel, and unable to manage the economy.

Trump's business experience enabled him to push the right buttons to get the economy going, and this was accomplished despite Democrats in Congress blocking his every effort for change. The Democratic Party bonded together to block any legislation to implement Trump's ideas to improve the economy.

In addition to the Democrat blockade, many top Republicans opposed Trump. The Bush family refused to support Trump's campaign, and none of the Bushes attended the Republican Convention. John McCain and Mitt Romney, former Republican nominees for president, turned into Trump haters and refused to attend the convention. Kasich and Rubio had disagreements with Trump, and scratched the

the convention. There was a split in the Republican Party, with several top Republicans against Donald Trump. Mitch McConnell and Paul Ryan, the Senate and House leaders, also had disagreements with Trump, and both were against the drain the swamp idea.

Changing the Washington environment was a goal of Donald Trump because he was not a politician. Trump believed legislators should serve a short time, and pass the baton after a few years in office. This idea was against the established rules where politicians could remain in office as long as they could be reelected. Both Democrat and Republican legislators were dead set against his drain the swamp program.

The Republican anarchy against Trump was unusual because the leaders of the party had professed for nearly eight years that they needed help from the White House to pass their conservative legislation. President Obama had vetoed all Republican statutes, but Trump's drain the swamp focus went against the politicians' plans to stay in office as long as they could gain reelection. The entire Washington establishment disagreed with the idea of limiting time in office, and worked behind the scenes against Trump.

Several high-level Republicans also had a personal dispute with Donald Trump, and this was another problem. Romney and McCain were critical of Trump during the entire election. This was somewhat understandable with McCain since he was known for lack of loyalty. However, Trump had supported McCain when he ran for president in 2012, so the switch was unusual. Romney was another story; Willard "Mitt" Romney and Donald Trump had similar backgrounds, although Romney was a politician and Trump was a real businessman.

Both Romney and Trump were born into wealthy families, and had advanced degrees from well-known universities. Romney's father, George Romney, was CEO of American Motors, and he grew up in *Motor City.* George Romney was also Governor of Michigan from 1963 until 1969, so Mitt Romney had politics in his blood. His loyalty came into question when he voted against the auto bailout in 2009; after all, he owed his wealth to the automobile business. Mitt Romney also had business experience as a consultant with Bain and Company, although Bain was known to be a school for Harvard MBA graduates with no business experience.

Donald Trump was also born into wealth, and graduated from the Wharton School of Business at the University of Pennsylvania, an Ivy League school. His business experience was more hands-on than Romney's in that he was successful in the tough New York construction business. Trump's business experience was blue-collar, and Romney's white-collar. Loyalty is probably the biggest difference between the two; Trump is known for strict loyalty, and Romney is famous for being tricky. Neither Romney nor McCain's disagreements with Trump had any effect on the election, although both tried their best to prevent his election.

The media was persistent in their criticism of Donald Trump right from the beginning. The Pew research showed that 93% of the media reports were negative toward Trump during the entire election. The media bias is understandable since the press had announced their support for Hillary all along. However, the bias was so anti-Trump that the media made a point of criticizing Trump while leaving the other sixteen Republican candidates alone. The reason that Trump was the media target was probably that Donald Trump was the only candidate who gave more than he took from the media. Trump began calling the media *fake news* and the moniker stuck. Fake news is the new description of the mainstream media, but the voters hate fake news. The more conservative news channels like *One America News* and *Fox News* are the only news outlets that actually report the news.

Donald Trump had mistrusted the media and the polls for years, and the misgivings continued throughout the 2016 election process. He had often been misquoted even when the supposed journalists had taped his statements. The media anti-Trump process continued and Trump used the term *fake news* when discussing the media. He also called CNN the *Clinton News Network* because of the continuous anti-Trump reports.

The public accepted the fake news idea and began to distrust the media. The fake news situation turned against the mainstream media when the public agreed with Trump.

A September 2016 Gallup poll showed that the respect for the media had dropped to the lowest level ever recorded. The distrust of the media caused the television ratings of CNN, NBC, and ABC to fall dramatically. The *Washington Post* and *New York Times* support also declined.

Donald Trump ignored the mainstream media during the election; during the primaries and presidential election process, he sold his ideas directly to voters, without using the media, the RNC, or the pollsters. His direct communication approach was one of the primary reasons that he won the election. Trump communicated with voters with his nationwide rallies that attracted thousands of voters, even though the media failed to show the huge crowds on television. The attendees were insistent that Trump was their candidate, but the media refused to accept that their most unfavorable candidate was attracting so much attention. Trump's system worked, much to the chagrin of the media.

The media had been predicting a big win for Hillary for four years, and continued with this theme right up to election night. The pollsters also were predicting a Clinton victory with some polls showing Hillary's lead to be 30 points. Both were also dead wrong. The obvious question is how could these *experts* be so wrong?

The inaccurate media and poll predictions had a significant effect on the Democrat campaign strategies. Decisions as to which states Hillary would visit, and the amount of money to be spent on television advertising depended on the polling data. As it turned out, many of these decisions were precisely wrong because the polls were flawed. Hillary failed to mention this point in her book *What Happened.*

Donald Trump did not trust the polls and his intuition was right on. Trump understood the media and polling bias and used this to his advantage. Hillary and the DNC believed the polls, and this helped her lose the election.

Many pundits criticized trump's anti-media posture, but it actually was an advantage rather than disadvantage. The media bias led the Democrats to overlook the change in voter attitude in the mid-term elections. Donald Trump recognized that voters were unhappy and included major economic changes in his platform. Voters were tired of the Obama weak economy and false job promises, and wanted to take their country back.

The disastrous economy was a major factor in the election but the Democrats were sailing along on the Obama propaganda that the economy was great. How could any intelligent person believe that an anemic 1.7% GDP growth rate was great? The nine million workers unemployed knew better, and so did their neighbors. Hillary's plan to continue with the Obama policies was a monumental mistake – voters wanted a change. This *minor point* was also missing in Hillary's book.

Although the media claimed that Trump was not very smart, he was actually a genius in developing his campaign strategy. He did this himself and it worked. Some of his staff people like Steve Bannon took credit for directing the campaign plans, but Bannon's ego psyche failed; Trump developed his campaign strategy a year before Bannon got involved. Donald Trump may not be a politician, but he is brilliant in reading voters and developing plans to meet their needs. He did this better than Hillary and his sixteen Republican opponents.

Trump is also a brilliant negotiator. His skill must be innate, although he certainly fine-tuned this negotiating expertise during his years working with New York politicians and unions in his construction business. Hillary lacked this negotiating skill as evidenced by her lack of performance while dealing with foreign countries as secretary of state. Trump's negotiating skills helped him win the presidency.

Donald Trump used a direct communication approach with voters and it allowed him to avoid the media bias and connect with voters. Trump's unique ability to connect with people was a definite asset that helped him win the election.

Hillary never did connect with voters; she always preached as if she knew more than they did. The inability to listen to voters and adapt her campaign was a major problem.

The silent majority was looking for a candidate with the same ideas they had, and Donald Trump was their nominee. Anyone who attended the Trump rallies could easily see that the crowd was enamored with Trump. The media failed to take notice, or probably, *refused to take notice.*

The media always discounted the huge attendance at the Trump rallies, and Trump challenged the media to scan the audience with their TV cameras, but they never did. My wife and I attended a Trump rally in Detroit, and had to stand in line for several hours to get inside. While standing in line we noticed that many of the people had UAW jackets on, and were joining with executives in discussing Donald Trump. UAW leaders were absent, but the workers were there – big difference from prior elections.

The Trump rallies were really something to behold; the attendees were shouting *USA – USA*, and *Jail Hillary.* The passion and enthusiasm of the people was so obvious that the *fake news media* must have noticed. The charisma of the audience was magical.

The media experts missed the direct communication link because they were still thinking that Trump could never be an acceptable presidential candidate. The refusal to recognize the reality that Donald Trump was swaying voters was an error of judgement that continued the media prejudice. It is hard to believe that the media was so stubborn; they allowed their preconceived ideas to affect their judgement. It is difficult to understand how the so-called reporters could not notice the magnetism in the audience.

The media bias and one-sidedness were the dangerous elements that caused reporters to miss the important issues of the election. The anti-Trump jihad got in the way of reality.

Even after Trump won the presidency, the mainstream media maintained that Donald Trump was not *presidential;* they refused to accept the voters' decision, and closed their eyes to the election.

One wonders why the media is so anti-Trump. The media liberalism must be the answer since the anti-Trump rhetoric began when Trump announced his candidacy, and continued throughout the election process. Even after he won the election, the anti-Trump hot air continued despite his accomplishments.

There has been an amazing turnaround in the economy that the press refuses to acknowledge. Immediately after the election, the stock market took off and had reached record levels nearly 100 times in Trump's first eleven months. The Dow Jones Industrial Average was 18,259 on November 8, 2016, and topped 25,000 January 4, 2018, a record-setting 37.3% increase. The market started a downturn in January 2018, but the market rebounded, and consumer confidence was the highest in decades.

GDP growth increased to 4% stimulating the economy and jobs increased dramatically – workers could work. The stock market reached all-time highs despite the 2018 downturn. These are amazing statistics, but the media failed to report the results. Ignoring the superb financial results in the President's first year is trivial and foolish, but the media continue with the anti-Trump theme.

The failure to report the fantastic economic news demonstrates the media bias, but also shows that the mainstream media distorts their reporting with *fake news.* After nine years of recession economics, and the dreadful Obama administration's economic policies, the great financial reports should be front-page news. The failure to report accurate news has caused the voting public to question the media. The Pew research report indicates that the media has reached an all-time low in public opinion.

President Trump's foreign policy changes have solved the North Korea nuclear threat problem. He imposed strict import controls and negotiated with China to do the same. Trump threatened to bomb North Korea when Kim Jong Un threatened to send nuclear missiles to the U.S. The rocket man backed down, and announced he was stopping his missile tests, and would stop his nuclear development if the U.S. would not bomb North Korea.

The ending of the North Korea nuclear threat will go down in history as one of the world's greatest political accomplishments, and the media ignores it. Pundits are recommending the Nobel Peace Prize for President Trump.

The FBI attempted to fix the election for Hillary, and this was the first time in the nation's history that a government agency attempted to fix an election. The FBI actions did not become public knowledge until after the election, and Congress started another investigation.

Comey, and many top-level FBI officials were against Donald Trump, and did everything they could to slant the election. Comey doctored up the fictitious Russia dossier to obtain an illegal warrant to spy on the Trump campaign office during the election.

The FBI spying on Trump's office was similar to the Watergate scandal of the 1970s, but was much worse because it involved the courts, and the FBI. The entire Washington fraternity was against Donald Trump. Even President Obama was involved by monitoring the FBI actions against Donald Trump.

Fortunately, the FBI was unable to tilt the election to Hillary. After the election, Comey was still determined to damage Donald Trump, and used the false dossier to justify the Special Counsel investigation of the President. Despite his actions being illegal, Comey used every underhanded tactic available to defeat Trump.

SPYING ON AMERICANS
OBAMA SURVEILLANCE INFRINGED ON PRIVACY RIGHTS
SPECIAL REPORT

The FBI spying on Trump's campaign office made Watergate, the worst political wrongdoing in history, look like child's play, but was only the tip of the iceberg. Comey also gave Hillary a *get out of jail card* on the email scandal, and was instrumental in having a Special Counsel appointed to investigate the President. The FBI also failed to investigate the infamous Uranium One pay for play by the Clintons. Hillary was instrumental in giving 20% of U.S. uranium to a Russian firm after Russia donated $145 million to the Clinton Foundation

The Clintons were successful in hiding their Russia involvement in the Uranium One acquisition until the Peter Schweizer' book *Clinton Cash* was published in 2016. Schweizer covers the Uranium One deal, the Clinton payoff, and Russia obtaining the nation's uranium.

The FBI also used the fake news dossier to begin an investigation of Trump, but after two years of inquiry, there has been no evidence found of any Russia collusion. Mueller also found no evidence of any Trump-Russia involvement. The entire government attempt to find some Trump connection with Russia failed.

Hillary started the Russia scheme with her drive to tie Trump to Russia. Russia had threatened Obama during the 2012 presidential election, and Hillary believed that targeting Donald Trump with a Russia connection would be a great way to damage his chances even though the *dossier* was proven false.

The silent majority could see through Hillary's smokescreen and ignored the fake news. Despite all the FBI and CIA behind the scenes illegal actions, and Hillary's Russia fairy tale, Donald Trump survived.

The FBI and Special Counsel investigations of President Trump still continue despite absolutely no evidence of any connection between Trump and Russia. There is definitely evidence that Hillary was paid for her vote to approve the Russia Uranium One acquisition, but the FBI and the Special Counsel have not investigated Hillary or Bill Clinton.

The FBI investigation had proven Hillary guilty of mishandling classified material on her private server, but Comey let her off scot-free. He reported that Hillary willfully mishandled classified information with her email server, but allowed her to avoid prosecution with his judgmental decision that *no reasonable prosecutor would bring such a case.* This decision was not his to make, and Comey was fired for overstepping his authority on the email investigation.

Illegal Spying on Trump

The entire FBI involvement in the election was illegal, and the American public has lost respect for the agency. How can the top U.S. investigation agency be so involved in the political arena? The new Attorney General, Jeff Sessions, has started a program to clean up the FBI and the action is certainly overdue.

The Washington bureaucracy was determined to do anything and everything to get Hillary elected, even if illegal actions were required. The FBI, CIA and the other intelligence agencies used illegal behind the scenes activities to sabotage the Trump campaign including illegal spying on the Trump campaign office.

Congress is now investigating the illegal *Spygate,* but if the inquiries are like the Benghazi investigations that took years and resulted in absolutely nothing, there is little hope that any action will be taken. It is tragic that our government is able to illegally spy on citizens and get away with it without any accountability.

The entire primary and election process was for Hillary and against Trump. The mainstream media selected Hillary as their candidate when she left the secretary of state office in 2013, and never wavered in their support.

The media jihad was so strong for Hillary that many Americans accepted that Hillary would win because they heard the prediction every single day for over three years. Evidently, the jihad believed in the axiom, *if you tell people the same thing over and over they will eventually believe it.* A hundred different polls predicted a Clinton victory.

The inaccuracy of the polls has never been explained. The sample audience often included more Democrats than Republicans and caused polling errors. The sample audience must include an equal number of Democrats and Republicans for the results to be accurate.

Voters lost respect for the polls since they were so obviously slanted toward Hillary. The pollsters should at least issue a report explaining why they were so wrong if they are to be important in the future. Trump paid no attention to the polls, but the DNC and Hillary used the polls to plan their campaign strategy.

Washington politicians were also for Hillary and against Trump. The Democrat claim that Trump was *not presidential* became a daily theme. How that idea ever became popular is a mystery since Donald Trump took *center stage* in every debate, and handled himself more *presidential* than his competitors.

Will Rogers' comment on politicians was *I don't make jokes, I just watch politicians and report the facts.* The people claiming that Trump should not be a candidate because he was not a politician failed to understand that voters wanted a non-politician.

The anti-Trump rhetoric started when he announced his run for president on June 15, 2015, continued thru the primaries, the election, and the post-election period. Past presidents, including George Washington, have been criticized by the media, but never like the media jihad against Trump. Washington's war record was even criticized in the newspapers of the 1700s, indicating just how irresponsible the media can be.

Reporters are often reckless in their articles, and their editors fail to hold them accountable. The editors are also irresponsible; no one holds them accountable either. The media jihad is reckless in their reports on Donald Trump, but they underestimate his ability to fight back.

No other president has been successful in handling the negative press. Some have had the support of the media, but those under fire have suffered. Even though Bill Clinton was a media favorite, he sometimes suffered severe criticism. George W. Bush was often criticized, but he failed to fight back. Obama never had any negative media coverage because he called it racist. Obama was an expert in claiming racism whenever the media attempted to criticize him.

Donald Trump is the only winner in the media vs the president war. He immediately began calling the mainstream media reports fake news, and the name stuck. Fake News has become part of the dictionary because of Trump. He gained the support of the silent majority when the fake news became so delusional. Most Americans are against the media today, and this is a major change in our media environment.

The spreading of news was almost nonexistent until Johannes Guttenberg invented the printing press in 1439. The first newspaper was the *Notizie Scritte* (written notice) published in Venice in 1556, but the paper was biased in their reporting. Newspapers around the world continued with biased reporting, but many readers ignored the prejudice.

Newspapers remained the primary news reporting function until radio began covering the news in 1920. Detroit radio station WWJ began reporting news on August 31, 1920, and radio news became popular. Ted Turner started 24-hour cable news reporting in 1980 with CNN, and cable news began to take over news reporting. The 24-hour cable news networks were a mixed blessing; while reporting 24/7, the news was insufficient to fill 24 hours unless a major disaster occurred. Immediate news reporting became available, but the networks began reporting their opinions to fill up the time. The news reporting became repetitive, and all channels covered the same news.

Unfortunately, biased news reporting became the norm with cable news channels. The bias is obvious, but the media ignores the issue. While Ted Turner was a genius, he created a system that quickly went haywire.

The public is enamored with cable news, and 24-hour news reporting grew to be a giant industry. Some radio reporters like Rush Limbaugh are still popular, but radio and newspapers have disappeared into the background in news reporting. However, cable is as biased as *Notizie Scritte in 1556.*

The media jihad picked up where the Venice newspaper left off. The reporting by the mainstream media was so biased that most Americans gave up on receiving accurate news. Trump's fake news accusations hit a nerve with the public, and many people stopped watching the cable news channels. Several liberal newspapers also saw a decline.

Trump's fake news stance defeated the media jihad and completely changed the way the public viewed news reporting. They no longer accepted the biased reports as gospel, and questioned every piece of news. Americans have become news analysts instead of news watchers accepting everything that is reported by cable news. Trump's perseverance with the fake news counterattack won the media jihad war.

After winning the presidency over impossible odds, Donald Trump has continued the direct approach to voters, completely ignoring the media. The public agrees with his *fake news* claims, and the media lost its trustworthiness.

Many Americans tired of the continuous anti-Trump rhetoric and bias, and have tuned the media out. The TV news channels are suffering with their audiences, and their ratings have declined dramatically.

While free speech and a free press are guaranteed by the Constitution, the continuous release of unverified data is rampart. The Russia *dossier* is in the news daily despite being immediately recognized to be false. The dossier is a joke, but is being used by the media to attack President Trump.

People fail to recognize that over 90% of the journalists are ultra-liberal, and journalists fail to accept that their overt bias is shredding their credibility. The mainstream media has very little believability with the American public, but the pompous media attitude doesn't allow them to recognize their problem.

Journalists continually go *over the line* when covering President Trump, but their editors are even worse. Over 90% of the *New York Times* and *Washington Post* editorials are negative toward the President, and the papers continue with their bias even though their volume has dropped significantly.

The daily White House press conferences prove the media bias, with most of the reporter's questions being anti-President Trump. The press also fails to report the Trump administration successes with the economy, foreign policy, immigration, and energy. Their bias is so apparent that the newshounds sitting in the press conference looks the same. It a like a Norman Rockwell painting. The White House press conferences have lost their popularity because each is a repeat of the prior day's discussion.

Many people simply ignore the mainstream media and use the remote to change channels to tune them out. If they can find a reporter they trust, they listen, but as soon as one of the anti-Trump liberals appears, they immediately change channels. The egocentric reporters failed to recognize that their audience had completely ignored them; they live in their own pompous, opinionated world.

The media bias caused them to ignore that voters had changed their thinking on politicians, and began voting them out of office in the mid-term elections. How the media missed this is anybody's guess, but their bias must have been a factor. The silent majority had simply had enough of Obama's policies and weak economy.

It is incredible that politicians, the media, and the pollsters ignored the silent majority movement. You would think that at least one element would have noticed that times were changing. Hillary missed it, but Donald Trump recognized the situation, and used it to his advantage.

Trump saw that the public wanted change, and used his business experience to develop a campaign platform that included fixes for the nation's problems. Jobs were an issue for voters, and he pressured industry leaders to stop shipping jobs over the border. Even before his election, Carrier and Ford cancelled plans to move plants out of the country; truly an amazing accomplishment by Donald Trump that the media ignored.

Trump also started a trade policy to make products in America. The Japanese had used currency devaluation of the yen to increase sales of their products in America. The result was a loss of many U.S. companies and a huge loss of jobs. The camera was primarily a U.S. product, but the business has been lost to Japan.

The exchange rate problem caused the closure of U.S. plants and job losses in automotive, camera manufacturing, electronics, machine tool, and construction equipment businesses. Politicians failed to understand the disastrous job losses, and did nothing to fix the problem.

It is difficult to understand why Congress ignored the import problem; evidently, politicians do not understand how important manufacturing is to the country. Without manufacturing, the nation loses jobs. They may not understand manufacturing, but they should understand business.

Industry executives complained to the government agencies about an uneven playing field, but politicians failed to act. Either they did not understand trade, which is a distinct possibility, or lobbyists controlled them, which is also possible. Whatever the reason, Congress did absolutely nothing to stem foreign imports and the resulting loss of jobs.

The trade issue became a key campaign issue that American workers understood, but politicians failed to accept. Hillary must not have understood either, because she continually touted NAFTA and the Trans-Pacific Partnership trade agreement as being great for the country, despite the trade deficits and job losses. The trade imbalance issue had been ignored for over sixty years, and the nation lost five million manufacturing jobs after NAFTA was approved.

Donald Trump recognized that job losses were a serious problem and an issue with voters, and developed a plan to fix the problem. The trade imbalance and resulting job losses were not campaign issue with any of the candidates except Trump. Trump made jobs and trade key elements of his platform, while Hillary stuck with promoting current trade agreements.

Donald Trump's business experience in the New York real estate market taught him the negotiating and deal-making skills that can correct the trade deficits. He called the bureaucrats who had signed the trade deals idiots, and he was right. Trump's campaign speeches in which he criticized government negotiators as being stupid were right on.

Trump revealed the U.S. trade deficits in his rallies, and voiced the need to stop the loss of jobs to foreign countries. The trade deficit with China is $350 billion, Japan $70 billion, and $65 billion with Mexico. While these countries are trading partners, there should be a more equitable trade balance. The interesting point is that Hillary failed to understand trade imbalance to be a problem. Washington politicians had ignored the issue for decades, and Hillary was playing the same tune, while Donald Trump made trade a key issue.

Donald Trump developed his campaign platform with little help from advisors or consultants. His experience and background gave him the ability to develop programs to fix the country's problems. Trump used his rallies to listen to people and get their ideas on key voter issues. His quick mind enabled him to see solutions for the issues, and develop a campaign platform that would attract voters. The main difference between Hillary and Trump's campaign visits was that Donald Trump listened, while Hillary preached. Simply watching the campaign speeches proved this point.

The general opinion that the Trump victory was a massive upset and shock to Americans is not only overdone, but is a fallacy. The Democrats, the media, and the pollsters were obviously shocked and considered Trump's victory a major upset, but this group is in the minority compared to the 140 million voters in the 2016 presidential election.

There was a change in voter thinking prior to the election, and the Trump victory was no surprise to the silent majority. They had made their opinions known in the 2010 and 2014 elections, but Hillary and the DNC ignored the results. The voters wanted a change, and Trump was to be that change.

Donald Trump was the only presidential candidate who understood the change in voter attitude. He paid no attention to the media or the polls, but did pay attention to voters who attended his rallies. The direct communication between Trump and the voters was the key to his success. The constant poll results showing a Hillary win were dead wrong, and the pollsters have never explained why. However, one poll asked a unique question: *How will your neighbor vote?* Evidently, some individuals were afraid to say they would vote for Donald Trump because of the constant media reports that Hillary was a sure winner. When asked how their neighbor would vote they expressed their true feelings. Strange way to get a true answer, but this particular poll was more accurate than the other 100 polls.

The continuous media bias favoring Hillary distorted the poll results in many cases. However, there must have been errors in sample size and the questions asked because over 90% of the polls were wrong; some were even reporting that Hillary was leading by 30 points the day of the election.

The media prejudice in reporting that Hillary was a sure bet probably affected the answers given to pollsters; the liberal mind-set in the nation was also a factor in the distorted poll results. The polls were wrong for two years and everybody but Donald Trump assumed they were accurate. The polls were not only wrong, but dead wrong. Most of the polls were reporting a sure Clinton victory up until midnight on election night. The inaccuracy of the polls remains a mystery, but they certainly affected the Democrat strategy. Unfortunately, for Hillary, the polls told a story they wanted to believe, and led to poor decisions by the Hillary campaign team.

One poll reported a 40-point lead for Hilary, which was obviously a huge error. There is absolutely no way polls can be that far off if the sample audience is reasonable, and questions are structured properly. It is obvious that the pollsters were wrong, but the question is whether bias toward Hillary played a part. While there has been little criticism of the polls, the errors must be addressed if the public is to believe polling data. Following the election, poll errors were omitted from the hundreds of reasons given for Hillary's loss, and even Hillary did not blame the polls in her book – she did blame everybody else, but not the pollsters. The poll data has not received any attention by the media so the answer may never be known.

250

The articles and books written after the election fail to mention the weak Obama economy as one of the reasons for Trump's victory. The 2008 housing recession was the worst financial crisis since the Great Depression of the 1930s, and the government caused both economic debacles. The Federal Reserve caused the depression by raising interest rates in 1928 causing the stock market crash in 1929. Congress caused the 2008 housing recession with years of legislation to increase home ownership for minorities. The government caused both disasters, but refused to accept responsibility.

The government efforts to fix the Depression and the 2008-2009 housing recession failed miserably and the nation suffered for years with the economic disasters. President Obama always bragged that he fixed the economy, but the recession continued throughout his eight-year reign. GDP growth, the best measure of the economy, was a recession- era growth rate during his eight years. Obama used *Jobs* as his keynote in several State of the Union speeches but his performance in creating jobs was the worst of any president. The number of people in the work force declined 5% during his administration.

Job Creation by Presidents

President Obama's *jobs program* failed miserably, but President Trump's plan created more jobs than the prior three presidents. He simply knew how to get things done. Most of Trump's campaign promises had to do with improving the economy and creating jobs. Despite the Democrat opposition wall, the President was able to accomplish most of his campaign promises during his first year.

Donald Trump, the *outsider,* identified the problems and developed fixes for the economy. Hillary was touting a great Obama economy during the campaign, ignoring the unemployed, and underemployed. The business executive and outsider fixed the economy.

President Trump's Economy

The mainstream media has failed to cover the increase in consumer confidence, the job increases, and the overall improvement in the economy, and the miraculous foreign policy actions. For the first time in decades, worker pay is increasing, and companies are paying bonuses. Solving the North Korea nuclear threat was a stroke of genius.

In addition to the economy improvements, the situation in the Middle East has taken a turn for the better. Trump promised to kill ISIS, and the military is well on the way to make this happen. President Trump lets the military do their job, and they don't drop leaflets telling terrorists where the next bombs will strike.

The President's success in foreign policy have also been ignored by the media. The elimination of the North Korea nuclear threat will go down in history as one of the world's greatest feats in foreign policy. Unfortunately, the media does not report the Trump accomplishments, and Americans are unaware that we are finally winning the war in the Middle East, and the North Korea nuclear threat has ended. What a ridiculous situation. Our cable news networks only report their jihad fake news – unbelievable. Where is Walter Cronkite when we need him?

The FBI Spygate was illegal, and the CIA underhanded tactics failed to stop Trump. Washington politicians pulled every string to damage Trump, but the string broke. The media jihad used every trick in the book to destroy Donald Trump, but the dreadful tactics also failed to work. Trump's opponents threw everything but the kitchen sink against him, but he not only passed the test, he came out on top.

Trump's victory was amazing considering the Obama administration attempts to fix the election for Hillary. The unethical actions failed, and the silent majority elected Donald Trump the President of the United States.

CHAPTER SEVEN
HILLARY CLINTON

Hillary Clinton

After fifteen years of chasing the presidency, Hillary expected to win the office. The FBI and media did all they could to help, but she still lost. After leaving the White House as first lady in 2001, she spent the next fifteen years running for president, but lost to Obama in 2008 and Trump in 2016. Her book *What Happened,* giving her analysis of the election revealed her inability to recognize her problems that caused both losses. Hillary is simply not electable, but she ignores it.

Everybody has ideas as to why Donald Trump won the presidency, and the topic will probably be debated for years. The articles and books written on the subject talk around the reasons for Trump's victory, but none report that Hillary simply had too many personal problems to be elected. Hillary Clinton was actually unelectable because of her baggage. Another problem is that she refuses to accept that she has baggage; she blamed everything on the *right wing conspiracy.*

Hillary Diane Rodham Clinton was born in Chicago on October 26, 1947. She was the daughter of Hugh and Dorothy Rodham, and was raised in the Chicago suburb of Park Ridge. Hugh Rodham graduated from Penn State University in 1935, and played for the Nittany Lions football team. He was a staunch Republican, and managed a fabric business in Chicago. Hillary's mother Dorothy was a homemaker.

Hillary graduated from Yale Law School in 1973. She met Bill Clinton at Yale, and after marriage in 1975, moved to Arkansas. She worked for the Rose law firm in Little Rock. Bill Clinton won election as the Attorney General of Arkansas in 1977 with a salary of $26,500. Hillary earned $24.500 at Rose. The combined income of $51,000 was slightly less than the $12 million they earned in 2001 when they were *broke* according to Hillary.

Hillary has a tendency to exaggerate; when she told reporters that she *landed under sniper fire* in Bosnia, videos showed the landing was uneventful. New York Times writer William Safire called Hillary a *congenital liar.* Lack of truthfulness would turn out to be a major problem during the election.

Bill Clinton was elected Governor of Arkansas in 1979 at age 33, and the Clintons attempted to increase their net worth in a real estate investment project called Whitewater Estates. Hillary was the legal counsel for the venture.

The Clintons joined friends Jim and Susan McDougal in a real estate investment plan to sell lots on a 230-acre plot of land on the White River in Arkansas. They borrowed $203,000 in 1979 to begin the project, but interest rates increased to 20%, and the real estate project failed. The Clintons lost $69,000.

Bill Clinton was involved in an illegal loan of $300,000 to Susan McDougal, and she served 18 months in prison for contempt of court. The loan scandal became a problem for Bill Clinton, but

Susan McDougal protected him by refusing to answer questions. The judge sentenced her to two years in jail for contempt, but she remained silent. She was released after 18 months, and Clinton pardoned her when he was President.

The *New York Times* published an article during the 1992 presidential election about the Clinton Whitewater dealings that led to an Independent Counsel investigation of Bill and and Hillary Clinton. The investigation discovered several illegal actions in the Whitewater deal, but the Clintons were able to avoid prosecution. The Special Counsel subpoenaed Hillary's payroll records from the Rose law firm during the investigation, but the records were never found.

Shortly after the statute of limitations expired, Hillary found the payroll records in the White House. She evidently had been walking around the box of payroll records for years. Hillary used the *right wing conspiracy* excuse, but the public refused to accept it. The Whitewater lie became her first piece of baggage.

The Special Counsel later dug into Bill Clinton's involvement with Monica Lewinsky, an intern in White House when Bill Clinton was President. The Lewinsky scandal seemed to last forever, and was daily news. Bill Clinton denied under oath that *I never had sex with the woman,* but Monica Lewinsky presented her dress that proved him a liar. Independent Counsel Kenneth Starr determined that Clinton was guilty of perjury and obstruction of justice. The actions were felonies, and the House of Representatives started impeachment proceedings.

The House approved impeachment, and the process went to the Senate. A two-thirds Senate majority vote was required to remove Clinton from office. Bill Clinton was impeached, but Senate Democrats refused to vote him out of office, and he remained President.

Only two presidents have been impeached in the nation's history; Andrew Johnson in 1868, and Bill Clinton 130 years later in 1998. Richard Nixon was threatened with impeachment during Watergate in 1974, but he resigned the presidency before he was impeached.

Both Nixon and Johnson suffered with a loss of political support, and lost credibility with the public. Bill Clinton sailed through the impeachment with little criticism from his Democrat supporters, and remained popular.

Bill Clinton was always thought to have a Teflon coating because he continually avoided his many scandals. The Teflon worked, and saved him a lot of grief after impeachment. It was as if it never happened – amazing.

During the Monica Lewinsky scandal, Hillary attempted to protect her husband. She had protected him in prior sex scandals, but the Lewinsky-Bill Clinton scandal was a proven fact, and it occurred while he was President of the United States.

Hillary accused Monica Lewinsky of aggressively going after her husband, but the facts proved otherwise. Her attempts to help Bill Clinton were ignored, and made her appear to be against women. Another piece of baggage was added to Hillary's backpack.

The Whitewater and sex scandals are still a black eye for Bill Clinton. Whitewater was later made into a television series that appeared for several weeks in 2018. The Clintons have been successful in dodging prosecution for scandals over the years, but impeachment was one they were unable to avoid. However, the Clinton Democrats simply ignore Whitewater, Lewinsky, Paula Jones, and impeachment.

Hillary's loss to Obama in 2008 was a shock; she had been touted to be the next president for years. She had been the first lady, a senator from New York, and supposedly had the experience, but Barack Obama easily beat her. This should have been a warning that Hillary was overrated. How could she lose to a candidate who had little or no experience in politics? Obama had never even had a job. The Democrats were so enamored of Hillary that they accepted her loss as a temporary setback.

Hillary was still determined to be president. She studied the 2008 campaign to determine why she lost, but failed to recognize that the Clinton scandals were a big problem. Hillary continued to use the right wing conspiracy excuse whenever a scandal was mentioned. Hillary simply refused to believe that she could have been the problem.

Hillary is not electable. The media and Democrats failed to understand that voters simply do not trust Hillary Clinton. Of course, Hillary will never admit to being unelectable, and this is her biggest weakness. She continually blames everybody and everything for her problems, when she should look in the mirror.

She possibly could have improved her electability after the loss to Obama, but even after she researched the loss, she failed to see that voters do not trust her. Polls showed that 70% believe she is a liar. Hillary simply cannot see that her lack of truthfulness is a problem.

Her research into why she lost to Obama was an excellent attempt to understand the cause of the loss, but evidently, Hillary allowed her personal feelings to get in the way. She refused to accept that she could have been the reason she lost.

The Democrats and the media were blind to the problem, and continued to push for Hillary's nomination. The media had a jihad against Trump, and a crusade for Hillary. Despite the age-old Whitewater and Benghazi scandals, and the email disaster, the media did all they could to get her elected in 2016.

Beginning in 2013, the media touted Hillary as the first female president. Even though she had accumulated considerable baggage, the media ignored the problems. The female vote was supposed to carry her through the election, but the female vote she received was far less than she expected.

Female voters failed to show up in sufficient numbers for a Clinton win. She did win the female vote, but the 54% majority was not enough. Hillary supporters still claim a victory with women voters, but Trump received far more female votes that the experts predicted.

The polls echoed the media push for Hillary, and the returns continually predicted an easy victory. The public was constantly reminded that Hillary was to be the 2016 Democrat nominee, and was almost a sure winner in the presidential election. The media barrage was really something; it was as if the media were using the *illusory truth* idea that if something repeated enough, people will believe it.

The propaganda was so overpowering that some Republican voters were afraid to admit to pollsters they would vote for Donald Trump. This fear of being noticed as non-Hillary caused many people in the polling audience to refuse to admit they would vote Republican, and this affected the poll results. The Trafalgar poll attempted to avoid this error by asking *who will your neighbor vote for?* An unusual question, but the poll was one of the most accurate because the individuals expressed their true feelings.

Hillary announced that she would be a 2016 candidate for president on April 12, 2015 – at least she avoided April Fools' Day April 1 – a day for playing jokes. This was her second time to run for president; her first announcement was made on January 20, 2007 for the 2008 election. She was also the media favorite in the 2008 election, but lost to Obama, the candidate who emerged from the Chicago Democrat machine.

The announcement was expected since the media was enamored of Hillary. Women were certainly excited about her running because she would be the first female President of the United States.

The constant favorable forecasts by the media and the polls made the DNC and Hillary overconfident, and affected their campaign strategy. She decided to ignore public opinion that the economy was a disaster, and followed Obama's propaganda that he had saved the nation from the 2008 housing recession.

The economy during Obama's eight years was the worst post-recession period in history. The prior post-recession GDP growth rate averaged over 5%, and was 10% in one case. During Obama's eight years, the GDP growth rate averaged 1.7% - an utter disaster. Obama was the only president in history who failed to have a GDP growth of 3% in any period during his presidency. The GDP growth during the Obama reign was a recession-era rate; the 2008 recession continued until Donald Trump was elected President.

It was astounding that Hillary, the DNC, and Democrats refused to accept that the financial crisis was still affecting the economy. The indicators were there, but they ignored them. Trump was well aware of the problem, and paid attention to the voters who attended his rallies. The economy was the primary difference between the Democrat and Republican parties.

Despite the Obama claims that he had pulled off a miracle, and saved the nation from the financial crisis, there was record unemployment, and homeowners had not regained their home equity. The silent majority recognized the recession was still gripping the country, but President Obama refused to accept the disastrous financial reports. Hillary's campaign strategy of continuing the Obama policies was a mistake, and another element that drove voters to Donald Trump.

Hillary still fails to recognize her error with the economy during the primary and election periods. The economy was a key issue with voters, but Hillary fails to list the financial crisis as an issue in her book. As she travels around the world attempting to sell her book, Hillary continues with her rhetoric about losing the election. The number of people who caused her loss has increased to 36, but the economy still fails to make her list.

Hillary blames her loss on everybody in her book; she must have maintained a diary of every comment that people made during the election. She even blamed the media – her longtime ally, and the FBI, who broke the law in their attempt to help her win. Trump's Russia connection was on page one of her book, but the anemic economy was not included.

There were four other Democrat candidates in the race. Bernie Sanders a Socialist senator from Vermont, Martin O'Malley, the Governor of Maryland, Lincoln Chafee, Governor of Rhode Island, and Jim Webb, former Senator from Virginia. Hillary was always predicted to be the nominee; the polls indicated a 30-point lead, and the media had already picked her as the winner.

Bernie Sanders, a little known senator from the small state of Vermont, was a surprise. He won the New Hampshire primary with his Socialist giveaway program – he promised everything free, with no plan to pay for anything. Hillary attempted to match Bernie's giveaways, but always fell short. During the primaries, Bernie was able to beat Hillary in many contests, and this certainly was an indicator that Hillary had a problem. Voters noticed, but Democrats failed to pay attention.

Hillary soon recognized that Bernie was a real threat, and decided to eliminate him from the race. The Democratic National Committee was the solution to the Bernie Sanders problem.

Obama had left the DNC $25 million in debt after the 2012 election, and Democrat leaders had been unable to raise donations to get back in the black. The DNC was spending $4 million a month on the 2016 campaign, and was close to bankruptcy.

The Clintons saw an opportunity to take over the DNC, and offered to help with the finances. Hillary gave the DNC funds, but demanded that the organization allow Clinton people to run the operation.

Debbie Wasserman Schultz was the DNC chair, and was under fire. She resigned, and was replaced by Donna Brazile, a strong Clinton supporter. Brazile was the person who gave the questions for the CNN debate during the primaries to Hillary *before* the debate. Brazile was one of the CNN commentators and had access to the debate questions. The mainstream media ignored the underhanded tactic, and the public knew nothing about it.

This was unheard of in presidential debates, although it happened in TV shows in the 1960s. Participants in the $64,000 game show were given the answers before the show. The game show scandal shocked the world, and executives were fired. However, Brazile's feeding the debate questions to Hillary was kept a secret. Of course, the Clinton scandals were always kept secret.

The Clintons took over the finances of the DNC and reorganized the operation with their people in charge. Controlling the DNC funding allowed Hillary to cut off money from the Bernie Sanders campaign, and he soon dropped out of the race. Surprisingly, Bernie took the defeat graciously, and immediately supported Hillary's campaign.

Bernie had been critical of Hillary throughout the primaries, and his quick support of Hillary raised eyebrows. Another surprise was that Bernie immediately paid off his $40,000 credit card bills that were overdue, and his net worth doubled to one million dollars. Apparently, money changed hands.

Hillary had eliminated the Bernie Sanders threat to her nomination, and even though the drop out was a shock to most, the media let it slide. Bernie went away quietly, and pundits wondered if there was a payoff involved; Bernie had personal financial problems that went away almost as quickly as his chances of being president.

The media did not pursue the reasons for Bernie's quick departure; they were happy that their candidate had prevailed. Both the polls and the media upped their predictions of a Hillary victory. The takeover of the DNC by the Clinton organization was truly a stroke of genius. It eliminated Hillary's only real opposition to the Democrat nomination.

Meanwhile Donald Trump was winning the Republican primaries, avoiding the personal attacks by his opposition. Hillary soon realized that Trump could very well win the Republican nomination, and he became another threat to her election. The Clinton machine decided that they had to do something about Trump, and they went into action.

Hillary and the DNC paid $12.4 million a dirt gathering firm Fusion GPS to dig up anything they could to damage Trump's chances. The Clintons supplied all the dirt they could dream up, and gave it to Fusion's Christopher Steele, a former British spy who had worked in Russia.

The DOJ helped Hillary in selecting the Fusion firm. A top DOJ official, Bruce Ohr, was involved with Fusion; his wife Nellie actually was on Fusion's payroll, and furnished the Clinton dirt to Christopher Steele

Steele knew Russia from his prior work with M16, and it appeared to be a good subject since Obama was threatened by Russia in the 2012 election. Hillary approved the Russia topic, and Steele went to work. Hillary's plan was to claim that Donald Trump colluded with Russia to damage her chances for election.

The documents were called the dossier and the first memos were released in the summer of 2016. However, when experts reviewed the papers, they found that the individuals reported to be in meetings with Trump were nowhere near the locations, and the individuals denied the accusations. In fact, many were in other countries. Steele's sources were unidentified, and the experts concluded that the Hillary Russia dossier was a total fabrication.

Steele was initially unable to sell the Clinton-Russia dossier since the media rejected the document. Even the media jihad failed to publish the dossier at first.

Hillary received help from John McCain, a fierce enemy of Donald Trump. McCain sent an aide to England to obtain copies of the dossier, and spread copies to the FBI, CIA, and Congress. Since McCain was a Republican, and a respected senator, his influence brought attention to the dossier, and this was an amazing stroke of luck for Hillary.

FBI Director Comey immediately passed the dossier through his friends and it ended up with the *New York Times* and *Washington Post,* the Trump-hating newspapers. The Hillary dossier was picked up by the media jihad, and the Trump-Russia topic became everyday fake news. The Russia-Trump issue would become the main topic of the election.

It was a near miracle that the Hillary funded Russia dossier became the Democrat and media jihad golden goose for the election. Once the media began to raise the Trump-Russia matter, Hillary started using the dossier in her campaign. The Russia topic snowballed into the biggest fake news in history.

James Comey used the dossier to spy on the Trump campaign office. He doctored up the fake dossier, presented it to the FISA court, and obtained a warrant to spy on the Trump campaign. The FISA court is limited to *foreign intelligence* and does not have authority to spy on American citizens, but the FISA judge allowed the spying on Donald Trump.

The Watergate spy tactic of the 1970s was the worst political scandal in history, but the 2016 FBI spy case topped Watergate. The FBI spying on Trump was illegal, but the illegality did not bother FBI Director Comey. He was determined to undermine Donald Trump any way he could.

The Russia dossier suddenly became the most important part of the election. The media jihad used the dossier ad nauseam, and Democrats accused Donald Trump of fixing the presidential election. Of course, the entire Russia issue had no credibility but that small problem did not matter to the media jihad. Not only did Russia become the single most important issue in the 2016 election, Trump-Russia continued to be the prime media and Democrat matter throughout 2017 and 2018. The dossier paid for by the Democrats as a political attack on Donald Trump became the colossal news item for three years – unbelievable

Hillary paid a questionable source, Christopher Steele to create a false paper accusing Trump of colluding with Russia. The dossier was immediately proven a fabrication, and was discounted by experts who checked the document. A typical Clinton piece of *dirty politics* suddenly became the most important issue in the election.

The Clinton machine had done an amazing job of creating a ghost parable that was full of baloney, but the fake news dossier became a favorite tool for the media jihad. Fortunately, the silent majority could see through the dossier drivel, and paid little attention to the media and Democrats in the voting. The Hillary-Russia dossier, despite all the attention, had little effect on the election results. The silent majority could read between the lines.

The Russia nonsense did not stop after the election. Democrats used the dossier claim that President Trump was connected to Russia as the tool for constant criticism. The intent was to use the Trump-Russia issue to impeach the President.

The Hillary email scandal was another problem that never went away. The former secretary of state destroyed over 30,000 emails *after* they were subpoenaed. Hillary used a private server and cell phone to communicate, despite government rules requiring the use of government-issued servers. She claimed this was just a *convenient* method of communication, but few believed the excuse. Hillary's intent was to *control* her email library to hide any documents that could damage her candidacy. However, *after* the emails were subpoenaed, she was forced to destroy the 30,000 that could be a problem. Hillary used professionals to destroy the emails, and the documents became invisible. This was no accident; it was an intentional violation of the law, and Hillary knew very well that it was illegal.

Not only were the emails deleted, Hillary destroyed her server and cell phones, an amazing and illegal action. This was kept secret by Comey and friends, and only surfaced later when an FBI informant presented the facts.

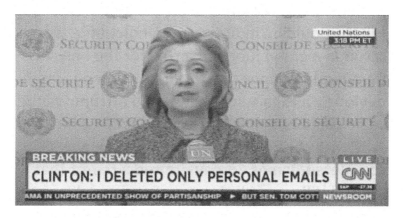

FBI Director Comey was in charge of the email investigation, and the FBI found over a hundred classified documents in Hillary's *personal* emails. The investigation also found evidence of *criminality*.

An unreported fact is that Federal law requires prison time for these offenses. The use of a private server and cell phones was against State Department rules, but Hillary was determined to hide her emails.

The results of the FBI investigation were not made public during the primaries. Comey and the FBI investigators found that Hillary had violated the law with her personal server handling of classified material, and had lied to the FBI about the emails. Both offenses were felonies and required jail time.

Comey was required to report the facts, and Hillary would be indicted. The indictment would result in a grand jury and a trial for the only Democrat nominee for president. Comey was obviously a Hillary supporter, and a Trump hater, so he could not allow this to happen.

Months before the FBI investigation was completed, James Comey drafted a report that cleared Hillary of all charges. Comey had obviously made the decision to allow Hillary go free before the investigation was complete. However, the draft included the statement that Hillary was *grossly negligent* in handling classified material.

276

On July 5, 2016, three weeks before the Democratic National Convention, James Comey called a televised press conference to report the results of the FBI investigation of the Clinton email debacle.

His initial remarks were extremely critical of Hillary, accusing her of mishandling 112 classified documents on her private server, and pointing out the seriousness of the offense. He was also critical of her use of the private server and cell phones. It appeared that Hillary was going to jail. However, the picture changed completely.

Comey reported that in his opinion, Hillary did not *intentionally* break the law, and *no reasonable prosecutor would bring such a case.* Based on the facts of the case and the FBI investigation, this was an amazing conclusion. Incidentally, Comey changed the term *grossly negligent,* to *extremely careless.*

Comey was responsible for the *investigation,* but did not have the authority for prosecution; that was the job of the Justice Department.

The bottom line was that Comey refused to indict Hillary for her email crimes, and enabled her to continue running for president. This was his intention from the beginning of the investigation.

The entire FBI investigation of Hillary's emails was a sham. Comey was in charge, and determined right from the start that Hillary would not be prosecuted because the Democrats would be without a presidential candidate. After so many years of Democrats touting Hillary as the front-runner, how could Comey upset the apple cart? He accomplished his objective, but it would later cost him his job.

Congress, as usual, was asleep at the wheel. With oversight responsibility, legislators should have been involved in the FBI developments if they were to be effective in limiting the damage. Congress finally began an investigation of the FBI actions during the email investigation in 2017.

This was obviously too late to change anything, and the investigation went nowhere because the FBI refused to cooperate. The agency simply refused to release any records. The FBI ignored the congressional oversight committee subpoenas. Congressional oversight was ineffective in both the Benghazi and the email scandals. The Hillary email issue was a matter of national security, but the FBI and CIA refused to cooperate, and refused to give documents to the congressional subpoenas – unbelievable.

The 30,000-email problem became front-page news, even though the mainstream media attempted to ignore the issue. Hillary claimed the emails had to do with her Yoga exercise classes; the public did not buy the excuse, but it was better than the age-old *right wing conspiracy* statement.

Hillary's use of a private server and cell phone for emails when the other members of government adhered to the government protocol was intentional. She simply wanted to control her written documents. Hillary always thought she was above *normal people,* and the email business was just another example of her *attitude.* As usual, she got away with it; other people would be in jail.

Hillary was simply hiding emails she did not want anyone to see. She planned this right from the beginning, and her method of destroying emails was a well-planned action; she used electronic experts to destroy the *personal* emails.

FBI Director Comey allowed Hillary get away with using her private server to handle classified documents. He even drafted the document clearing Hillary of any criminal activity months before the investigation was completed.

The Clinton machine had avoided prosecution many times in the past, and was again successful in dodging responsibility for the email fiasco. The Clinton Teflon dust always works, and the double standard for the Clintons continues. Comey certainly helped hide the debacle.

Hillary mentions the email disaster in her book, but obviously avoided talking about Comey's mysterious conclusions about her *intentions.* The email scandal added to her baggage, and despite the Comey reprieve, the baggage got to her during the election. Based on her book, Hillary actually believes that she has no baggage. All criticisms are due to the right wing conspiracy. This caused her to lose in 2008, and caused the loss to Trump.

Hillary also blamed the FBI for causing her to lose. This is an unbelievable accusation because the FBI prevented Hillary from going to jail on the email issue. FBI Director Comey stretched his authority in claiming that Hillary did not *intentionally* violate the law when she mishandled classified data while she was secretary of state. Comey also ignored that she was guilty of perjury by lying to FBI agents, a felony that requires jail time.

James Comey proved to be a disreputable person during the election, but he was guilty of attempting to *help* Hillary, rather than hurt her. He even put his job on the line by illegally spying on Trump. This got to him later when President Trump fired him for his actions during the election. Hillary's claim that Comey had hurt her chances was certainly disloyal to her main supporter. Of course, Hillary had never been loyal to anyone but herself.

The top FBI officials were guilty of interfering in the 2016 election, and their activities were illegal. The agency is supposed to remain neutral in elections, but the agency was far from neutral in 2016. Comey and his Deputy Director Andrew McCabe were fired for their involvement, and several other FBI agents were demoted. The new FBI Director Wray has a major job on his hands to clean up a disorganized agency. It would appear that new people are necessary at all levels of the FBI organization.

The nation's top law enforcement agency has lost all credibility, and should be completely reorganized. The FBI hasn't done anything since assassinating Bonnie and Clyde, and the public thinks so little of the agency that a name change may be in order.

There is a lack of *intelligence* in the intelligence agencies; both the FBI and the CIA are supposed to be intelligence agencies, but have missed the big intelligence issues during past years.

Both agencies missed the Japanese attack on Pearl Harbor in 1941 despite obvious evidence of the attack. They also missed the attack on the World Trade Center in 2001. The CIA and FBI gave *student visas* to the 21 terrorists to develop flying skills without checking their background. The CIA even claimed that Saddam Hussein had weapons of mass destruction, despite U.S. and U.N. inspectors being unable to find any weapons after two years of inspection. The CIA actually caused the war in Iraq.

The U.S. intelligence agencies have failed to do the job for at least the past seventy years, and the intelligence operation should be reorganized. For some unexplainable reason, there are sixteen intelligence agencies, and nobody can determine who does what, if anything. The all spend most of their time keeping secrets from each other.

Government officials lied to Congress during the 2016 election. James Clapper, former Director of National Intelligence lied to Congress, when questioned about the FBI involvement in the 2016 election, and should be in jail. John Brennan, the CIA Director, also lied to Congress, and should be right behind Clapper on his way to jail. Comey's lies were too numerous to count, and even though he was fired, he should be next in line for jail time.

The remaining intelligence agencies receive less public attention, but they evidently don't do very much because we don't even know who they are.

Both the CIA and FBI agencies were against Donald Trump during the election, and used their influence to aid Hillary. Both agency actions were illegal, and the top people lied to Congress. No wonder the silent majority has lost confidence in the corrupt intelligence agencies.

Despite the help of the FBI, CIA, and practically everybody in Washington, Hillary's lack of veracity proved to be a big problem. People simply did not believe her. Hillary also made serious errors in her campaign strategy.

She went along with the Obama economic policies despite the poor economy, and her overconfidence led her to make mistakes in her plans to visit key states during the campaign.

Hillary failed to recognize that voters were trending toward Trump in the rust-belt states, and she did not focus on those prime electoral states. Wisconsin, Michigan, Ohio, and Pennsylvania, traditional blue states, voted for Trump, and the electoral votes turned the tide. Her confidence in winning the rust-belt states led her to avoid visiting the states in the final days of the election; she flew over the rust-belt states on her way to Wall Street.

Donald Trump visited all the rust-belt states in the final few days and won every state, although the margin was less than one percent. The states switched to Republican for the first time in recent history. When Wisconsin gave its 10 electoral votes to Trump, it pushed him over the 270 votes required. If Hillary had obtained just one more percent in the rust-belt states she would have won. Hillary evidently failed to recognize the mistake because she ignored this in her book.

Hillary demanded a recount for some of the rust-belt states, but the recounts confirmed the Trump victory. Hillary's overconfidence led her to believe the rust-belt states were in the bag, and they were, but they were in Trump's bag.

Another fact that has never been reported is that the media and the polls, with their ongoing predictions that Hillary was a sure winner, actually helped Trump win. The constant media and poll predictions that Hillary would win caused the DNC and Hillary to be overconfident, and led to mistakes.

Hillary also made other mistakes during the campaign. Her attempt to split the potential Trump voters, and gain additional votes, backfired. Her comment during a September 2016 media interview was a classic. The expression *you can take Trump supporters and put them into two baskets. There are what I call deplorables – you know the rapists and haters, and the people who are drawn because they think somehow he's going to restore an America that no longer exists* was also *deplorable,* and upset most voters.

Her *divide and conquer* strategy bombed out with her *deplorable* speech, since it was so insulting and offensive. It was exactly how she felt, but she should have toned it down a bit, because the comment received negative feedback for weeks, and certainly did not cause Trump followers to switch to her camp.

The last part about the *American dream no longer existing* also hit a nerve with most Americans who still believed in the American dream. Donald Trump's *Make America Great Again* theme was the optimistic pitch that voters wanted to hear. The entire Hillary speech was so negative that it drove another nail into the Clinton coffin. Election night was less than two months away, and the last thing Hillary needed was a negative speech that hurt her chances.

When Hillary was first planning her strategy for the 2016 election, she spent considerable time analyzing why she lost to Obama in the 2008 primaries. The loss was devastating since Hillary was considered the favorite; similar to the 2016 presidential election, Hillary was thought to be the winner. However, Barack Hussein Obama won the democratic nomination with 2273 delegate votes compared to Hillary's 1978, and went on to beat John McCain, and become the first African-American to be elected president.

It appears that Hillary's research into the 2008 election loss to Obama did not help her in the 2016 election, because she made the same mistakes. Even though she was the media favorite in 2008, she lost, and the same thing happened eight years later. Hillary's research effort failed to identify her baggage, or she refused to accept it. In her 2016 book *What Happened,* she blames everybody else for losing the election. Her research into the 2008 failed to help because she ignored that the real reason she lost was her lack of truthfulness.

Hillary's list of people who damaged her chances of being elected in 2016 included President Obama, Vice President Joe Biden, Bernie Sanders, James Comey, and Valdemar Putin. She even blamed the media despite their continuous support for her election. After the election, her list of guilty parties grew; there are now 36 individuals on her list. Interesting that she still fails to blame herself.

Russia is listed as the main reason she lost, but evidently everybody was guilty of not supporting her campaign. It seems like everybody is at fault except Hillary. Accusing Comey was ridiculous. He was fired for doing everything he could to help Hillary by claiming she was not guilty of mishandling classified material in her email scandal. The blame game list continues to grow, but most people have tired of Hillary's excuses, and many hope she would just go away.

Evidently, Hillary thought Bernie was too rough on her by pointing out her lack of truthfulness. She mentions in her book that she *accepts responsibility* for losing, but she never mentions lack of veracity.

Her baggage accumulated over the years, and never went away. The Whitewater scandal plagued her as first lady, and the Travelgate issue was another faux pas, along with the promised health care program that failed. When Hillary accidently found her payroll records that had been subpoenaed during Whitewater in her White House bedroom shortly after the statute of limitation expired; this added to her baggage. Her lying became the norm; she even claimed she was under sniper fire when landing in Bosnia, but film showed the landing was uneventful.

As secretary of state, the Benghazi tragedy hit on her watch; Hillary blamed it on some video, and that was another falsehood. The Benghazi tragedy was a disaster with the death of Ambassador Stevens, and three embassy people. Hillary was never able to explain why she refused to provide security for the Ambassador, and his people, or why she refused to send military forces to help.

The Benghazi tragedy was a Clinton classic. First, she caused the debacle when she played the political correctness game. She was attempting to follow President Obama's 2012 presidential campaign strategy that assured victory in Iraq. Benghazi was a terrorist hotbed, but Hillary pulled all security out of the dangerous city despite the continuous requests for more security forces by Ambassador Stevens. The lack of security created the opportunity for the terrorist attack. Evidently, Hillary believed that security forces in Libya would give the *appearance* that Obama's position that the Middle East was under control was untrue – which it definitely was. Libya, Iraq, Syria, and Iran were actively fighting the U.S. in the Middle East despite Obama's claims to the contrary.

The September 11, 2012 terrorist attack on the U.S. facility in Benghazi, Libya came seven weeks before the 2012 presidential election. President Obama had made campaign speeches claiming his policies were winning the war in the Middle East and the terrorist attack would jeopardize his campaign. President Obama and Hillary blamed the Benghazi terrorist attack on some video that supposedly offended Muslims.

Both wanted to protect Obama's rose-colored statements that *he* had solved the Middle East war that Bush had started. He even called ISIS a *JV team.*

The infamous CIA had ignored the seriousness of Benghazi and agreed to the reduction in security. After the attack, the CIA decided to issue *talking points* to cover up the terrorist attack, blaming the two-day uprising on some video that offended Muslims. The video excuse that it was a *sudden response* to the video made no sense because the attack lasted two-days, and involved mortar fire, and rocket-propelled grenades. The sophisticated weapons would certainly not been available for an instantaneous response to some anti-Muslim video.

Benghazi Tragedy

The FBI, CIA's sister *lack of intelligence agency,* immediately arrested some poor guy in Hollywood thought to be the producer of the video. The individual was thrown in jail without a trial, and is probably still in jail. Nobody has heard from him since.

Hillary's second mistake was blaming the two-day *terrorist attack* on some video that nobody ever saw. The public had never heard of the suspicious video, and questioned why it would cause a two-day attack involving mortar fire and RPG weapons. The attack appeared to be, and was, an organized violent attack on the U.S. compound.

Hillary knew the attack was a planned uprising; an hour after telling the nation that the disaster was caused by a video, she emailed her daughter, Chelsea, that the attack was an organized al Qaeda operation. Her *normal* method of handling disasters was to lie, and she continued to shade the truth.

President Obama had U.N. Secretary Susan Rice to appear on five television channels explaining that the video caused the Benghazi attack. Rice also appeared before the U.N. claiming the video caused the Benghazi disaster.

The Susan Rice television appearances appeared to be overdone. As Shakespeare said in *Hamlet, The lady doth protest too much methinks.*

President Obama, Hillary, and Susan Rice, continued to claim the video caused the Benghazi uprising, and the death of Ambassador Stevens and three other Americans. The video excuse was becoming the main topic of the day, but the public was beginning to suspect that there was more to the story.

Hillary's third mistake was lying to the families of Ambassador Stevens, Sean Smith, Tyrone Woods, and Glen Daugherty. She continued to tell the families that the video caused their deaths even though she knew this was a fairy tale dreamed up by the CIA. This act by Hillary and Obama goes beyond lying; it was a tragic hiding of the facts from an Ambassador's family.

The failure to fix the disaster she created in Benghazi was another sad occurrence. There were security people an hour away from Benghazi and instead of immediately sending forces to save Ambassador Stevens, the security team was told to *stand down,* and failed to help. Stevens and Smith died of smoke inhalation and could have been saved if the security force had immediately gone to rescue them. The lack of any military action to save the Americans killed in Benghazi remains a mystery. The CIA order to *stand down* was another attempt to prove that security and military action were not required since Obama had reported his strategy was winning the war. The *political correctness* actions had gone too far.

Hillary's final act in the Benghazi debacle was to demand that the security forces that were finally sent to help the embassy people in Benghazi, remove any riot gear. She felt that wearing riot gear and bulletproof vests appeared too *aggressive.* Hillary had never been on the front lines or in a terrorist situation, but any intelligent person would never, in a New York minute, even think riot gear was scary to terrorists who murdered innocent people every day. Hillary was playing the political correctness card again even after the Benghazi tragedy was over. Her Benghazi actions displayed her lack of sensitivity to Americans who lost their lives to terrorists. Of course, Hillary never, at any time, accepted that she was the cause the Benghazi debacle, but she pulled all security and that caused the tragedy.

The Benghazi debacle will go down in history as one of Obama and Hillary's most shameful errors. Obama's sole intention was reelection, and he ignored the death of Ambassador Stevens and three American citizens. Obama completely failed his responsibilities as President, and his so-called legacy will include Benghazi. Hillary acted as his *enabler* with her actions, and lack of action. Historians will nail both for their political actions, rather than doing their job.

Hillary was guilty with her unexplainable cancellation of security, lying about the video, refusing to allow rescue teams to visit the site, and refusing to allow riot gear for rescuers after they were finally deployed to Benghazi. Her lack of action on a tragedy she caused was tragic.

She lied throughout the disaster, but her lies to the Stevens family, and the families of the others killed in the Benghazi were disgraceful.

It is difficult to imagine a more callous act by government officials, particularly the President of the United Sates and his secretary of state. Benghazi was an utter disaster, and will go down as one of the worst *deceits* in the nation's history. Books will be written, and movies made that tell the tragic story.

A congressional inquiry committee started an investigation of Benghazi, but after five years, the committee has yet to issue their findings. The problem is that the key individuals, President Obama, Hillary, the military, FBI, and the CIA refuse to cooperate; all Benghazi records have been hidden, and classified as *military secrets.*

The members of the security team that were told to stand down by the CIA finally told the Benghazi story. Mitchell Zuckoff, a professor of journalism at Boston University, co-authored a book with members of the security team entitled *13 Hours in Benghazi.*

The book was made into a movie and describes in detail the harrowing Benghazi attack in which the CIA not only failed in *intelligence,* as the agency always does, but also covers the CIA stand down order that prevented rescue operations. The CIA, as expected, criticized the book because it did not fit their excuses or talking points.

The CIA refuses to make public the transcripts of communications between the top CIA official in Benghazi and his superiors in Washington. When the government, particularly the CIA and the FBI are in embarrassing positions, they mark everything *classified.* Even Congress has been unable to break through their wall; the CIA simply ignored their subpoenas.

Zuckoff is a respected author who has written three other books, and had no reason to damage the CIA. He co-authored the book with members of the security team who went through the terrible episode in Benghazi. His plan was to tell the public the true story behind the Benghazi tragedy. The CIA, FBI, State Department, and President Obama have been hiding the scandal for six years. It is amazing that even the congressional oversight committee was unable to obtain the real information on Benghazi.

When asked why the military did nothing to help the Ambassador and his agents, the generals had no answers. The lack of military action has never been explained. The most powerful nation in the world was unable to send troops to save the Ambassador – unbelievable. The truth about Benghazi will never be known.

The mainstream media was in Obama and Hillary's corner, so they obviously did not pursue the truth on Benghazi. Most Americans assume that President Obama was only interested in gaining a second term; Benghazi stood in his way, so he found a way to eliminate the threat. Lying about the ridiculous video was his way of avoiding criticism on his Middle East policies.

Hillary's actions during Benghazi were deplorable, and indicative of her persona; she is a compulsive liar, and has little or no empathy. Her answers in the January 2013 congressional foreign relations committee meeting on Benghazi when asked about the deaths of four Americans, including Ambassador Stevens, Hillary yelled out *What difference at this point does it make?*

The hard line and rude reply certainly pointed out Hillary's lack of compassion for the family members of the four Americans killed when she failed to provide security for the Benghazi compound. Hillary will say and do anything to avoid responsibility for a problem. This has been her method of operation since her days in

Arkansas. The Benghazi tragedy was a perfect example of her lack of truthfulness. Columnist William Safire's statement that Hillary is a congenital liar certainly was appropriate for the Benghazi incident. She has never been able to clean up her act on lack of veracity.

Hillary's scandals began in her Arkansas days, but continued throughout her career as first lady, as senator, secretary of state, and presidential candidate. The baggage hurt her chances more than she admits. It appears Hillary does not even recognize that she has baggage.

Hillary's Baggage

Hillary's accomplishments as secretary of state were limited to increasing the State Department travel budget. During her four years, she visited 112 countries; however, she didn't do anything. Hillary has such a strong fear of making a mistake that she delays decision making until it is too late to make a decision. When she finally makes a decision, it is always *politically correct,* but it never fixes anything.

Foreign policy during Hillary's tenure as secretary of state was the worst in history. Nothing was done on the Iran and North Korea nuclear threats. North Korea became nuclear capable, and launches missiles twice a month. Iran is on the way to nuclear capability, and is a dangerous threat to the world. Hillary's State Department policies will go down in history as an utter disaster.

Hillary's performance in the 2016 election was nothing to brag about since it was the most corrupt in history, thanks to Hillary's takeover of the DNC, and the illegal FBI Spygate.

The Hillary funded Russia dossier failed to deter Trump, but Hillary used the fake news dossier as worldwide criticism of the President. Hillary used her underhanded tactics to make the 2016 presidential election one of the most shameful in history.

After losing the election, Hillary continued to claim she *would have made a damn good president,* and toured the world on her book selling agenda telling the world how she was abused during the election. Everybody was against her, and she should have won. Even her women voters failed to help her enough. By 2018, Hillary had become a joke, and had lost her audience.

Her invention – the Russia dossier – was the biggest accomplishment of her life. The fake document was the main topic of the election and post-election periods. It was amazing how she avoided her record of Russia collusion, and threw the Russia ball into Trump's court. Both Hillary and Putin must be overjoyed at the political fallout over a false document. The news media make the dossier and Trump's tie to Russia the daily news nearly two years after the election. Democrats even threaten President Trump with impeachment because of the dossier.

Hillary had two chances for the presidency, and she fouled both up. Her baggage and lack of accomplishments got to her. She still has followers, and even if *the third time is a charm,* the third time will never happen. Hillary will fade away just like Ralph Nader.

CHAPTER EIGHT

SYNOPSIS

The actions of the Obama Administration and the Clinton machine made the 2016 presidential election the most dishonest in history. The Washington fraternity – the FBI, CIA, Attorney General, and the National Security Advisor - all played unscrupulous roles in the Shakespearean tragicomedy. Hillary Clinton played a leading role in the drama with her Russia dossier and the takeover of the DNC, but the FBI was the star by putting an agent in Trump's campaign office to spy on his strategy.

Hillary also hired Christopher Steele, a former M16 agent who worked in Russia, to develop a Trump-Russia document. Steele wrote 17 memos between June and December 2016 that became known as the *dossier.*

The first dossier memos were issued in June 2016, however, analysis proved the dossier to be a fabrication; the Russian individuals in the supposed meetings with Trump were actually in other locations when the meetings took place. Steele also used sources that were unverified, and the dossier was determined to be a fraud.

John McCain saved Hillary when he entered the comedy. McCain sent an aide to London to get the dossier, and passed copies to FBI Director Comey, CIA Director John Brennan, and members of Congress. McCain was an enemy of Trump, but since he was supposedly a Republican, the false dossier became breaking news. The mainstream media and Democrats immediately began touting the dossier as gospel. The media jihad picked up the dossier ball and ran with it.

However, a small problem developed with the Democratic plan to accuse Trump of collusion with Russia – voters could read between the lines, and voted for Donald Trump.

Democrats were outraged at the election results, and developed a plan to discredit the new president. The Russia dossier was the only tool the Democrats had in their anti-Trump toolbox. Hillary's forty years of baggage was a problem, and Obama's eight years were a disaster.

Democrat Senator Chuck Schumer and House Minority Leader Nancy Pelosi bonded, and were able to coerce the other 243 Democrats in Congress to build a wall between President Trump and the legislature. Schumer used the filibuster technique to delay every Trump appointee, and Pelosi made long anti-Trump speeches in the House. Some Democrats even threatened impeachment, but the impeachment claims were not credible.

The media also failed to accept the election results, and continued with their criticism of President Trump after the election. The Russia collusion matter was their ongoing theme. Their intense hate of Donald Trump did not end November 9, 2016, but grew stronger as the post-election days passed. The Russia issue continued to be front-page fake news. Never before have the media attacks on a president been so vicious.

The dossier started as a political attack by Hillary on an opponent, and was based on fallacious propaganda. The errors in the dossier were ignored by Hillary and the media, and used in their daily crusade against the President.

Democrats used the dossier after the election in their attempt to impeach President Trump even though the document included obvious falsehoods; the media continually proclaimed that Trump's actions in the dossier could be treason. The Democratic Party was grasping at straws with this effort, but continued to chase the Russia rabbit because they had nothing else. The entire Trump-Russia claim was a hoax.

Donald Trump won the presidency all by himself; he received little or no help from the Republican Party. In fact, The RNC was convinced he would lose, and on election night, was sending out emails saying *It's not our fault.* When the tide turned about ten o'clock on November 8, 2016, the chicken-hearted RNC members began to support Trump. Even slippery Paul Ryan and Mitch McConnell moved to Trump's corner when the reports of a possible Republican victory were announced on television channels.

The main reasons that Donald Trump was elected are as follows.

- Hillary is not electable – she has baggage.
- Voters demanded a change in Washington.
- Trump offered change – Hillary did not.
- Trump listened to voters – Hillary preached.
- The media and crazy polls aided Trump.
- Government attempt to fix election failed.

When voters elected Donald Trump, the Washington scene became a war between the Trump-voter team, the Democrats, and Republican turncoats.

Politicians, both Democrats and supposed Republicans were against Trump's idea of *draining the swamp;* the hand shakers wanted Washington to remain the same inefficient, unscrupulous, fraternity. Many Republicans in Congress even continued their anti-Trump crusade after the voters chose the non-politician to be the President of the United States. The traitorous legislators did not like the idea that Trump demanded that the Washington swamp be drained. Politicians wanted to stay in power, and objected to Trump upsetting the apple cart.

While the Democrat wall of opposition was a huge problem, President Trump had to deal with the hypocrites in the Republican Party. This was an unheard of situation, and made it next to impossible for the President to get things done.

Schumer and his Democrat senators were delaying *all* Trump appointments, and Pelosi's House Democrats were making speeches demanding impeachment. President Trump was forced to make the *Charge of the Light Brigade* all by himself; his lieutenants deserted him.

Trump's strong management style and strong personality, enabled him to get things done. His tax reduction law was passed after months of Schumer and Pelosi threats that tax cuts only helped the rich. The Democrat tag team was proven wrong when the middle-class received wage increases and the economy took off after the eight years of Obama economic hard times.

The President's foreign policy achievements were historic with his North Korea negotiations, and *killing ISIS* plan, but Schumer and Pelosi were critical, and accused Trump of being un-American, whatever that means. The media jihad refused to report the Trump wins, and the Democrats watching CNN failed to get the world-changing news.

The split in the Republican Party was evident as early as 2015. There were seventeen Republican candidates for president, and major differences in their campaign platforms were obvious right from the beginning. The candidates included governors, senators, and business CEOs, and all were capable people. However, they had different views of the nation's problems and solutions.

The five Democratic presidential candidates were not as experienced, and Hillary appeared to be the certain winner. However, a big surprise appeared when the primaries started; Bernie Sanders would turn out to be a popular candidate.

There would also be a surprise candidate in the Republican Party. The early favorites, Jeb Bush, Scott Walker, and Rick Perry, would fall out of the race early, and Donald Trump would take center stage.

Another surprise was the intense hate by the mainstream media against Donald Trump. The reason for the animosity has never been explained, but it was so profound that it turned into a jihad. While the media certainly preferred Hillary to a Republican, the dislike of Trump was passionate.

The 2016 election was the most corrupt in history with at least two government agencies, the FBI, and the CIA, using illegal tactics to get Hillary elected. The Director of the FBI, James Comey, was fired for his actions, and the CIA Director, John Brennan retired after lying to Congress. James Clapper, the Director of National Intelligence was also retired for lying to Congress. The agencies were famous for lying.

The intelligence agencies were also famous for *lack of intelligence,* and their attempts to destroy Donald Trump again proved their intelligence shortcomings - they bet on the wrong horse.

The media jihad has been going on for nearly three years, and the media hate crusade has continued after the election; in fact, it has been stronger. Their current actions are aimed at impeachment. The two-year FBI investigations and the Special Counsel are also targeting impeachment of the President.

The entire Washington political community is against draining the swamp; lobbyists, Trump's target during the election, are doing everything possible to discredit the President. Voters like the change in Washington, but politicians have the blinders on.

Prior presidents have suffered with the media, but the media hostility toward Donald Trump is the worst ever. Trump was successful in stiff-arming the media jihad with his fake news retaliation, and most Americans pay little attention to the mainstream media. Donald Trump is the only president who has been successful in beating the media. No other candidate could have survived the onslaught. However, the media jihad hasn't given up; the fake news couriers continue their anti-Trump efforts.

The Democrats formed their own wall against Trump after the election. The Schumer-Pelosi tag team immediately delayed all Trump appointments as long as they could, and this effort continues into 2018. The Democrats also rejected every piece of Trump's legislation to damage his presidency. The Democrats hope they can cause enough discord to impeach Donald Trump. Never in the nation's history has the opposing party caused such disorganization.

Democrats are simply anti-progress. They would rather damage the country in their attempt to gain power, rather than do their job as legislators representing their districts.

While Democrats and Republicans always differ on most subjects, the disagreements were massive during the 2016 election, and most issues remain unresolved.

2016 ELECTION ISSUES

- The economy
- Immigration
- Tax cuts
- Trade imbalance
- Obamacare
- Washington swamp
- FBI Spygate
- Russia dossier
- Hillary takeover of DNC
- DACA and Dreamers
- Fake News
- Democrat Wall against Trump
- Trump's Wall against Illegals

The only issue that was resolved by the election was Donald Trump's victory over Hillary Clinton. The political parties could not agree on anything.

Despite the importance of the twelve other issues, the Russia matter dominated the election and post-election periods.

Hillary paid $12.4 million for the fake news Russia dossier, and the false document became the big issue during the election. After the election, Russia remained the top political topic. As Republicans continue to say, *there is no evidence of any Trump connection with Russia, and* this is the naked truth – not politics.

The FBI has been investigating into Trump collusion with Russia for two years without any evidence of any Trump involvement with Russia.

The dossier was used to start a Special Counsel investigation of President Trump, but the yearlong Mueller investigation also failed to find any Trump collusion with Russia.

The Russia dossier was proven false by experts, but the media and Democrats continue to play the Russia tune. The anti-Trump factions continue with counterfeit claims of Trump collusion. There has never been evidence of any Trump involvement with Russia, yet the fairy tale continues sixteen months after the election.

It is truly astounding that a document invented and paid for by Hillary, prepared by a foreign intelligence officer that was proven to be a fabrication and untrue, became the main topic of the 2016 election. The media jihad succeeded in continuing the attacks on Trump with the fake news dossier to the point that many believe the falsehood. The old adage that if you tell people the same thing repeatedly, they will eventually believe anything, certainly applies to the Trump-Russia connection.

The entire Russia theme is simply Washington politics. A 2018 poll indicated that 90% of the public believed that the Russia claims had no validity, and had no effect on the election. The

Washington politicians continue to chase the Russia rabbit despite the facts. As Will Rogers said, *If you injected truth into politics, you have no politics.*

Despite Americans voting for Trump, the Democrats rejected the vote, and immediately built a wall of opposition. The election issues continued, and prevented the government from working; the Federal Government is at a standstill. The hate for the President was so vicious that some Democrats even made speeches in the House demanding impeachment, but the speeches were groundless.

The leaders of the Democrat Party, Senator Chuck Schumer, and Congresswoman Nancy Pelosi, bonded all members of the Senate and House to wall off President Trump. The President had to go into overtime to force Congress to *Make America Great Again* and pass the tax reduction legislation.

Despite the Democrat wall, and after months of congressional debates, President Trump was able to get tax reform passed. The tax cuts immediately started an economic boom, but Democrats refused to recognize the improved economy. Companies brought billions back into the country, and added jobs. Firms started paying bonuses to workers, and for the first time in decades, employee income was rising. Unemployment dropped to the lowest level in years, and consumer confidence pushed the stock market to record heights.

The turnaround of the economy was amazing, but Democrats continued with their age-old idiom that tax-cuts only helped the rich. The public knew better because their 401k reports were increasing every month.

The Democrat tag team, Schumer and Pelosi, ignored the economy advances, and their bitter attitude got worse. The Democrats also refused to recognize the President's astounding accomplishments in foreign policy. His victory over Kim Jong Un of North Korea will be recognized as one of the world's greatest diplomatic achievements. After the President threatened to bomb North Korea to stop their missile launches, Kim Jong Un agreed to stop all nuclear development if the U.S. would not bomb his country.

Democrats and the media also ignored the improvements in the Middle East, and the public was not getting the news. President Trump allowed the military to run the *war,* and ISIS was on the run. The Obama practice of dropping leaflets warning ISIS of the next bombing by the U.S. military was scrapped. The terrorists were gone when the bombs hit after the Obama warning.

The media jihad is puzzling; reporters simply close their eyes to reality, and refuse to accept the real world. They continue with their Trump jihad, ignoring the public's will, the President's accomplishments, and the fact that most of their customers have tuned them out. One thing for sure – the media jihad fails to cover news – they report their *opinion* of the news.

Trump attempted to pass legislation to build a wall on the southern border to prevent drugs and criminals from entering the country, but Democrats rejected funding. The Republicans also introduced legislation to cancel Obamacare, but Democrats continued to accept Obamacare despite the costs being double the estimate.

Schumer and Pelosi used DACA and the Dreamers as tools to reject Trump's wall. Their objective is to allow illegal immigrants to enter the country so they will increase the number of Democratic voters.

The media and Democrats never discuss the attempt to gain more Democratic voters with the illegal immigrant issue and for some reason Republicans are afraid to raise the voter issue. When Republicans object to illegal immigration, Democrats use their religious freedom and un-American claims.

The religious freedom claim does not hold true because immigration law specifically declares that only legal immigrants are allowed to enter.

The attempt to allow illegals to enter so Democrats can obtain more voters is never mentioned by the drive-by media. Republicans fail to counter the illegal immigrant and religious freedom arguments, and lose the immigrant battle. The immigration debate will never go away as long as Democrats continue to demand that illegal immigrants must vote.

The FBI involvement in the 2016 election was the first time in the nation's history that a government agency attempted to fix an election. The media fails to cover the activity, but the FBI actions were illegal, and the agency ignored the law. FBI Director Comey and his top people were so intent that Hillary be elected that they violated the law.

Congress began an investigation of the FBI in 2017 that could result in criminal indictments, and a few of the guilty individuals have already been replaced. President Trump fired Comey, the FBI fired Andrew McCabe, and several top-level FBI people were reassigned to lower-level jobs. The FBI has lost all credibility, and a complete reorganization is required. President Trump appointed Christopher Wray the Director of the FBI on August 2, 2017, and he has an almost impossible job to clean out the biased organization mess.

Despite absolutely no evidence of Trump's involvement with Russia after two years of FBI investigations, Comey doctored up the Russia dossier to obtain a Special Counsel investigation in May 2017. Robert Mueller was named Special Counsel, but the fact that he was previously head of the FBI made his appointment suspect.

As of April 2018, after nearly a year of the Special Counsel investigation, there is still no evidence of any Trump collusion with Russia. In February 2018, Mueller indicted 13 Russians for tampering in the 2016 election, but there was no mention of any Trump involvement. The indictments were meaningless since there is no chance that the Russians will ever go to court, but it satisfied the media demand that some action be taken. Putin claimed the individuals were not even Russian.

The Russia dossier is a classic example of the Clinton machine working behind the scenes. Donald Trump was a threat to Hillary's election, and a kill tactic was required to do away with Trump. The machine had disposed of the only Democrat threat by taking over the DNC, and stopping donations to Bernie's campaign, which caused Bernie to drop out of the race. The false dossier was intended to dispose of Trump, but voters rejected the biased fairy tale.

Hillary still claims that Trump collusion with Russia was the reason she lost the election. This thinking is impossible to understand because she invented the dossier – there was no accusation of any Trump-Russia connection before Hillary's dossier was developed. The document was proven false, yet was used by Hillary, the Democrats, and the media jihad, to attack Trump during and after the election.

An interesting caveat; Hillary is the one who has ties to Russia. The gift of 20% of U.S. uranium to a Russian agency happened on her shift as secretary of state. Uranium One, a firm owned by a Russia billionaire, *donated* $145 million to the Clinton Foundation, and Hillary recommended that the U.S. approve the firm's acquisition of an American uranium company. President Obama also approved the acquisition.

The Clinton pay-for-play transaction was kept secret for six years in typical Clinton fashion, and was not an issue in the election. Hillary was successful in putting the Russia matter in Trump's court despite being guilty of Russia collusion.

The Uranium One transaction and approval came under scrutiny in late 2017, and the DOJ began an investigation into the Uranium One deal. If the FBI is able to perform a nonpartisan investigation, the Russia matter will be a Hillary problem once the inquiry is completed.

Hillary also never mentions $145 million *donation* by the Russia-owned Uranium One to the Clinton Foundation. The only politicians connected to Russia are Hillary and Bill Clinton.

The ghost Russia dossier argument goes beyond reality. The dossier started the Russia-Trump claim without any evidence, and the document had been proven false. The fake news document not only was the hit of the election, but also became the driver for impeaching President Trump. Hillary and Putin must be laughing every time the fake news media discuss the Trump-Russia issue. Putin knew that Russia could not fix the election; his objective was to create havoc during the election, and with Hillary's help, accomplished his goal easily.

The 2016 presidential election was a debacle. The Clinton illegal actions, the FBI spying on Trump's campaign office, the CIA, FBI, and Hillary development of the fairy tale Russia dossier, caused corrosion of confidence in elections by the American public. Faith in the FBI, CIA, and the Justice Department dropped to the lowest level in history.

The faith in the entire government also reached basement levels. The division in the government created a divide that caused a complete halt in legislation, and Democrats held up the budget for nearly a year demanding amnesty for illegal immigrants.

The nation's 2018 budget year runs from October 1, 2017 to September 30, 2018. President Trump submitted the 2018 budget to Congress on March 26, 2017, but Democrats held up approval until February 9, 2018 – nearly a year later. However, Democrats are not concerned about approving the budget since they spend $500 billion more than the budget every year. Harry Reid, the Senate Majority Leader under President Obama, refused to approve a budget for *four years.* No wonder the public has given up on Washington politicians, and are demanding changes.

The hate for Donald Trump has never been questioned, or explained. The drive by Democrats to take power over the executive branch is understandable, but their animosity goes beyond sensibility. The media bitterness and hatred toward the President also goes beyond rational limits. The claim that he is not *presidential* never stuck, and his performance as President has been outstanding. The Russia conspiracy claim is based on the false dossier, and carries no weight.

However, the Democrat coalition continues to pound the President with Russia collusion claims, and make speeches demanding impeachment. The anti-Trump debacle is an attempt to denounce the President continuously until the 2020 election. The Democrats have nothing else to use in their goal of gaining the presidency. The Obama years were an economic disaster, and his foreign policy was even worse. The Obama foreign policies were a disaster, and President Trump has accomplished more in a year than Obama did in eight years. In fact, Obama has a minus F report card on foreign relations.

The continuous bashing of the President is wearing thin with voters. Democrats seem to forget that the American voters elected Donald Trump to be their President. Somehow, they forget this minor point. The silent majority ignores the anti-Trump assaults by Democrats, realizing it to be politics. The Democrat plan to criticize the President for four years could turn against them. The voters elected Donald Trump in 2016, and could very well vote for him again in 2020.

The FBI actions during the election were an atrocity. The agency is supposed to be non-partisan, but was totally biased against Donald Trump. FBI Director Comey doctoring up the false Russia dossier to obtain a warrant to spy on Trump's campaign office was bad enough, but using the dossier to start a Special Counsel investigation of Trump *after* he was elected certainly proved his hate for Trump. The CIA also used illegal tactics against Trump.

The media abuse of news reporting was contemptuous. The media jihad refused to report the news, ignoring the dramatic improvement in the economy, and President Trump's historical improvements in foreign policy. His forceful actions against North Korea caused a complete change in Kim Jong Un's nuclear missile program.

President Trump imposed strict restrictions on North Korea imports soon after being elected, and was successful in having China do the same. China is North Korea's main trading partner.

The North Korea leader began launching missiles over Japan and South Korea, both of which are America's allies. After Kim Jong Un threatened to launch nuclear missiles to the U.S. President Trump threatened to bomb North Korea into oblivion.

In April 2018, Kim cancelled missile testing, and agreed to stop nuclear weapon development if President Trump would not bomb his country. Trump eliminated the threat of nuclear war by the North Korea leader.

The media failed to acknowledge the President's miraculous accomplishment, and the public that watched CNN, ABC, CBS, and NBC, missed the news of the biggest foreign relations achievement since the fall of the Berlin Wall on November 9, 1989. However, the media jihad continued their drive to impeach the President – unbelievable.

Sadly, the 2016 presidential election will go down in history as the most fraudulent in the nation's history. Never before had the outgoing administration attempted to fix an election. While former President Obama has not been charged with involvement in the fix, his direct reports were involved, and it is difficult to believe that he was not the driver.

FBI Director James Comey was certainly the key player in the election fix, and even though he attempted to hide his illegal actions, his guilt is readily apparent, and he may very well be indicted and prosecuted.

CIA Director John Brennen lied to Congress and was forced to retire, but is still under investigation by Congress. Former Director of Foreign Intelligence James Clapper also lied to Congress many times and was forced to retire.

The entire government intelligence community was involved with illegal actions during the 2016 election; there must have been some direction from President Obama. It does not appear reasonable that the entire intelligence group would suddenly decide to fix an election. Proving this may be impossible because the agencies have marked incriminating documents *secret* to avoid prosecution.

Despite Hillary, the Clinton machine, the FBI and CIA, the Democrat wall, and the media jihad, Donald Trump was elected the 45th President of the United States.

The Inauguration

DATA SOURCES

All images and quotations are public domain.

Made in the USA
Columbia, SC
26 June 2018